WORKSHOP 2
by and for teachers

BEYOND THE BASAL

edited by
Nancie Atwell

HEINEMANN
Portsmouth, New Hampshire

Published by
Heinemann Educational Books, Inc.
361 Hanover Street   Portsmouth, NH 03801-3959
Offices and agents throughout the world

We wish to thank the following for permission to reprint previously published material: *16.00*

Page 32: "To Look at Anything" from *The Living Seed.* Copyright © 1961 by John Moffitt; reprinted by permission of Harcourt Brace Jovanovich, Inc.

Pages 34–38: Selections from "The Mountain Whippoorwill." From *The Selected Works of Stephen Vincent Benét.* Copyright 1925 by Stephen Vincent Benét, © 1953 by Rosemary Carr Benét. Reprinted by permission of Henry Holt and Company, Inc.

Every effort has been made to contact the copyright holders and the children and their parents for permission to reprint borrowed material. We regret any oversights that may have occurred and would be happy to rectify them in future printings of this work.

ISBN 0-435-08523-9
ISSN 1043-1705

Designed by Wladislaw Finne.

Printed in the United States of America
10   9   8   7   6   5   4   3   2   1

CONTENTS

ABOUT
WORKSHOP 2

*W*orkshop 2 is the second in a series of annual volumes written by and for teachers of grades K–8. Each *Workshop* addresses a current topic in the teaching of reading and writing. The theme of *Workshop 2* is Beyond the Basal.

Teachers who venture beyond the basal are still a distinct minority in North American schools. Basal reading series continue to dominate reading instruction in roughly ninety percent of our elementary classrooms. Recent published criticisms of basal programs (Goodman et al. 1988; Shannon 1989) have questioned the assumptions on which the programs are developed, among these that children learn reading in a sequential, systematic way, from parts to wholes, and that children learn reading in groups, all needing the same skills in the same order at the same time. In the basal scheme of things the teacher's role is to manage the program: to distribute, collect, and evaluate each group's workbooks, skill packs, and level tests. The publisher's role is to make all or most of a teacher's instructional decisions, to market and sell the basal program to textbook selection committees, and to reap huge profits from the commodity known as "the basal." As Patrick Shannon observed, "the odds are clearly stacked against teachers and students in American reading programs" (146).

The contributors to *Workshop 2* are teachers who have beaten the odds. They bypassed commercial programs to make literature, students' responses to literature, and the teacher's own knowledge the heart of their instruction in reading.

What do these teachers know? They understand that language

development is a process of refinement, from meaningful wholes to parts, that children's reading interests are idiosyncratic, that children's reading abilities are based largely on their diverse prior experiences with text. And, because they are themselves readers of literature, their goal is to create lifelong readers, not to exhaust the materials in the basal series. They understand that working through the selections in a basal or anthology bears no resemblance to the real-life situation of choosing a book according to personal need and taste, and enjoying it.

They are teachers who have done more than trade in their basals for classroom libraries of children's literature. As Kathy Matthews stated in a letter to me, they have come to terms with what they believe literature to be: "what purpose it serves in our own lives and how we want to extend those purposes to the classroom." They are known by their students as readers and therefore as teachers whose advice about reading will be artful and trustworthy. They have broken free of the basal version of what reading is and how teachers are supposed to talk about it.

Genuine literary conversation does not take the form of stilted questions that we would be embarrassed to ask of another adult. It is informal, authentic, open-ended, opinionated, and respectful of other readers. And it is comfortable. Teachers who know the pleasure of reading literature for themselves *relax*. They love reading, and they trust that students will find the same satisfaction as readers as they do. They ask questions that go beyond what is in the text—but always come back to it.

These are the teachers to whom children wish to apprentice themselves. Their students know that they are always ready to explore possibilities with books, that they will never work from old lesson plans or a teacher's manual, that they will read—and write—with children not to be models for them but because reading and writing are what this teacher does. A literature-based reading program "works" when it is founded on a teacher's immersion in literacy.

In a literature-based reading program, the teacher sets aside time in the classroom for students to be with books, to listen to works read aloud, and to respond independently. The teacher also introduces new authors, genres, texts, and styles of writing encountered in his or her reading. And the teacher accommodates young readers' choices of books. Only when children choose books do they get a full sense of what real readers do and what reading is good for. Their engagement with books that they have selected promotes the development of personal tastes in literature, personal styles of reading, and personal styles of response. Literature-based reading requires active readers who have literary preferences, just as a writer's workshop requires active writers with individual intentions and styles. Students who were raised on basals will need help adjusting to a classroom where personal response is the norm, where a teacher will ask them what they think about a literary work and why, rather than requesting a plot synopsis or the main idea—just as students raised on grammar worksheets and creative writing recipes need help adjusting to the autonomy and responsibility of a writing workshop. The contributors to *Workshop 2* have taken up this challenge.

In the lead article, Barbara Faust, the teacher of a combined pre-K and kindergarten in a public Montessori school, examines her own literacy in the light of five-year-old Stephen's love affair with a book. Barbara's knowledge of beginning readers and their literature has allowed her to broaden her definition of reading to include the whole range of rich literacy events that unfold in her classroom and enable even her youngest students to behave like readers. More importantly, Barbara's own love affair with literature has made her students *want* to behave like readers.

Cynthia Rylant contributes the Author's Perspective feature for this second volume of *Workshop*. Rylant is the author of *When I Was Young in the Mountains* (1982), *The Relatives Came* (1985), *Waiting to Waltz* (1984), and other books for children. In her provocative essay she explores how reading influences writers— how the art of reading literature is the best preparation for the art of writing it. Rylant observes that programs do not make writers or readers but that teachers who love literature can help children develop literary standards—and can take children's breath away with the beauty of written language.

In her memoir "Nebuchadnezzar Meets Dick and Jane," Ginny Seabrook, a teacher of grades seven and eight, remembers how she grew up loving books in spite of many of her teachers. Through the prism of her experiences as a reader, she examines her teaching and the changes she has made so that she might pass on her love of reading and her independence as a learner to her students. Ginny's reading history makes a compelling case for other teachers to reflect on and learn from their experiences as readers.

Marni Schwartz is also a middle school teacher—and an accomplished storyteller. In "The Silences Between the Leaves" she shows the power of one story in her life, beginning with an experience in the ninth grade. Through returning to the story again and again, Marni has come to know herself better and to understand how she fits herself to the world. She makes the point that when a literature-based program emphasizes wide reading, it may be at the expense of allowing children to discover key reading experiences in their lives.

Two of the contributors to *Workshop 2* describe students' encounters with literary genres other than the familiar "real life" literature most often found in classroom libraries. Kathy Matthews, a third-grade teacher, used mythology as a unifying theme in a year-long study of ancient civilizations. In "Responding to the Call" she explores the ways that Greek mythology served her and her students as a bridge to all of human experience. Her article is a joyful challenge to the culture-as-trivia approach of E. D. Hirsch (1987), as well as an affirmation of the abiding power of stories in our lives. Kathleen Moore's "Once upon a Time in Room Seven" tells the story of her second graders' encounters with fairy tales. These ancient stories bridged gaps between cultures, generations, and centuries when Kathleen and the children read the tales and researched their responses.

In the Author Interview, Kathy Hershey, a fourth-grade teacher from Centerville, Ohio, talks with Jack Prelutsky, who is surely one of our country's greatest ambassadors of poetry—because of his direct, contemporary language, because of his topics, which all children can see eye-to-eye with, and because his poems are funny and make the reading of poetry fun. It is evident in their conversation that, for Prelutsky, life itself is an art, to be lived to its fullest and captured on paper.

Cyrene Wells is a junior high teacher who based her reading program on my book *In the Middle* (1987). In her chapter she explores the role of audience in reading, specifically what turned up in letters that students wrote to each other about their reading and how peer correspondence allowed readers both to reflect and to "find voices that fit their audiences and audiences that fit their needs." Cyrene also acknowledges the danger of trying to adopt another teacher's approach without first clarifying what one expects will happen, and why. We watch as she stands back, takes a hard look at what is going on with her students, and takes responsibility for finding and solving her teaching problems.

Students' talk about books is the subject of Adele Fiderer's contribution to *Workshop 2*. Drawing on her experiences as a member of an informal reading group that met to discuss literature over dinner, Adele designed a model for her fifth graders to structure their own discussions about their independent reading choices. Their talk stimulates, focuses, and expands their thinking about literature, and fills their teacher's ears with the "passionate sound of readers in collaboration."

Carol Avery is the subject of the Teacher Interview, conducted in this volume by Jane Hansen. In Carol's first-grade reading program, *engagement with books* is the goal. There are no commercial reading materials, no ability groups, just Carol's collection of intriguing literature and her willingness to read stories aloud again and again, give her students time to be with books they have chosen, and talk with them about what readers do. Not surprisingly, Carol's students become readers. In the community of her classroom, literature is a way of life.

In "Children as Authorities on Their Own Reading," Bobbi Fisher, a kindergarten teacher, describes a reading program based on Don Holdaway's work in emergent literacy (1979, 1980). At the end of the school year, Bobbi interviewed her students about their experiences and attitudes in order to evaluate her program. The children's responses reveal their sense of autonomy as learners, their self-confidence, and their quite accurate sense of what they can and cannot do as readers. Primary teachers interested in alternative means of assessing reading abilities will be informed by Bobbi's approach to evaluation.

Dorothy Taylor, Joan Levy, and Rena Moore work with special populations of children. Dorothy's students are limited English speakers. In her search for appropriate reading materials, she turned to books written by the children themselves, in which predictable language patterns and topics of mutual interest served the children as a bridge to the published literature of their new country. Joan Levy and Rena Moore are, respectively, a special education teacher and a classroom teacher of grades two and three who joined forces to team-teach reading. Rather than remove special needs students from the classroom, Joan mainstreamed the children into Rena's literature-based program and then mainstreamed herself as Rena's partner in teaching reading. The demonstrated success of their approach raises serious questions about the structured, sequential methods advocated for special education students. When we deny any child literature as an entreé to reading, we divorce reading from its meaning and power—two elements that special students especially need.

Linda Rief concludes *Workshop 2: Beyond the Basal* with profiles of two of her literary apprentices, one aged four and the other fourteen. Jimmy and Tricia learned in the company of an adult who guides and directs them from her experience as a reader and writer. As a result both preschooler and adolescent turn to literacy for authentic purposes; they make it work for them in their lives as Linda does in hers.

Jimmy, Tricia, and the dozens of children who appear on the pages of this book have taken a cue from their teachers. In every case the teacher's orientation toward literature and acceptance —encouragement—of a diversity of opinions about the significance of literary texts have put children's responses at the center of the reading curriculum. The bookshelves are filled with literature, but in these classrooms *books need children* to give them significance. The literature-based reading program is geared toward what children can bring to the books, not toward what they are supposed to get from the books—and definitely not toward literature as the latest method for transmitting so-called reading skills invented by basal publishers.

As Kathy Matthews suggests, when we teach with literature, we must begin with the purposes it serves us as readers and how it might serve our students. In the end, I hope that we will surround children with literature because we cherish it and them, and because literature gives us a life that we wish them to know. When we look beyond the basal, let it be toward the ways that literature might illumine our students' lives and make them whole.

References

Atwell, Nancie. 1987. *In the Middle: Writing, Reading, and Learning with Adolescents.* Portsmouth, NH: Boynton/Cook.

Goodman, Kenneth, Patrick Shannon, Yvonne S. Freeman, and Sharon Murphy. 1988. *Report Card on Basal Readers.* Katonah, NY: Richard C. Owen.

Hirsch, E. D. 1987. *Cultural Literacy: What Every American Needs to Know.* Boston: Houghton Mifflin.

Holdaway, Don. 1979. *The Foundations of Literacy.* Portsmouth, NH: Heinemann.

———. 1980. *Independence in Reading.* 2nd ed. Portsmouth, NH: Heinemann.

Rylant, Cynthia. 1982. *When I Was Young in the Mountains.* New York: E. P. Dutton.

———. 1984. *Waiting to Waltz.* New York: Bradbury.

———. 1985. *The Relatives Came.* New York: Bradbury.

Shannon, Patrick. 1989. *Broken Promises: Reading Instruction in Twentieth-Century America.* Granby, MA: Bergin and Garvey.

*O*nly the rarest kind of best in anything
can be good enough for the young.
Walter de la Mare

STEPHEN AND
THE HAUNTED HOUSE:
A LOVE STORY

BARBARA Q. FAUST
Bennett Park Montessori Center
Buffalo, New York

I don't learn from children easily. The knowledge doesn't soak in gently the way water saturates a sponge. It's more like a dousing with cold water—I've accepted that.

I teach in a mixed kindergarten and pre-K classroom at a public Montessori school. In my literate community, we are all readers. Three-year-old Michael came to school one morning and asked confidently, "Do you want me to read you *The Pokey Little Puppy*?" His reading was a description of each of Gustaf Tenngren's illustrations. At first glance, Kyle's zoo story looked like Palmer method spirals; when he read it aloud it became, "In a dark, dark cave there was a . . . BEAR!" a story pattern Kyle had borrowed from Bill Martin, Jr. (1970a). Four-year-old Asherah stopped Jan, our assistant principal, and asked her if she'd like to hear *Dan, the Flying Man*; Asherah's reading was a memorization of a patterned text. It is all reading.

When I read aloud Judith Viorst's poem "Learning," the room erupted with gales of laughter and cries of "Read it again!" On another day Kyle and I learned together about how the ancient Egyptians used natron to preserve bodies when he drew on a book by Aliki to research mummies. And on another day we were all anxious to read Eric Carle's new book *A House for Hermit Crab* (we have four pet hermit crabs in our classroom). While reading it I was struck by its similarity to Leo Lionni's *The Biggest House in the World*. Each main character is an animal living in a shell; Carle's is a hermit crab, Lionni's is a snail. Although the texts differ, the illustrations are remarkably similar; each shell grows larger through the story. In a mini-lesson I used these

13

strong visual images to show the children how authors can confirm each others' work and see the world from similar perspectives. It is all reading.

We signal the start of a group share meeting in our classroom by winding a music box. One day, three-year-old Lauren gave me a note she'd written. "Will you read it to me?" I asked. She looked at the paper with her name at the top followed by eight lines of assorted letters. Solemnly she read, pointing to a letter here and there: "Lauren wants to wind the music today." "Great," I replied. "Can you put this on the message board so we can remember whose turn it is today?" (Harste, Woodward, and Burke 1984). It is all reading.

Early in the year, while finishing a conversation at the classroom door, I glanced back into the room. It was a transitional time; three children sat reading, and the others were milling about quietly. I returned to my conversation with Judy, the woman I work with. Seconds later, another glance—more children were reading. A final word to Judy, and I turned to the children to begin my planned lesson. "Wait, Judy," I whispered excitedly into the corridor. "Come look at this!"

All of the children were reading. There they sat—those readers. Some read to each other, some to themselves. Most read pictures, some read words—all read. While I had gone about my business, the children had gone about theirs, picking up books in the manner of any reader with a few minutes to spare. Their self-confidence, independence, and familiarity with many books that they loved made the choice to read a natural one. What did I do? I am also a reader, so I chose a book I loved and read. My lesson could wait.

Only readers choose books independently. Only readers read books independently. Only readers share books with friends. Only readers love books, which brings me to Stephen and *The Haunted House.*

A shy, thoughtful five-year-old, Stephen is in my all-day kindergarten. He treasures Bill Martin, Jr.'s *The Haunted House,* a title from our classroom library. One day, Stephen returned from the school library carrying another copy of the book, saying excitedly, "Look what I got!" He was thrilled to have come across a book he loved in a new setting. Shortly afterward I was given another book called *The Haunted House,* this one written by Joy Cowley. Stephen was the first person I wanted to share it with.

When he arrived at school that morning I called him over.

"Stephen, I have a new book I think you'll like. We can read it when you get back from breakfast." Stephen left the room but returned seconds later saying, "I don't think I'm goin' to breakfast. Can we read the book now?" I reassured him, "I'll save the book till you get back, I promise." He turned, walked a few steps and returned again, pleading, "Can we read the book now? I'm not goin' to breakfast." Finally realizing how important the book was to Stephen, I laughed and said, "Okay, let's read it together."

We sat on the floor and read the book six or seven times. After the third reading, Stephen pointed to an illustration of a suit of armor. "Remember this?" he asked. Several weeks earlier Stephen and Mujahid had used a book by Judy Hindley to research knights, and the armor was still familiar. When we had finished Stephen asked, "Can I read this by myself?"

"Sure," I replied. I watched as he sat on the floor reading and rereading *The Haunted House*. Then he got up, found his friends Adam and Mujahid, and offered to share the book with them. Soon all three were laughing over the "Oo-oo-oo-oo" and the "Woo-oo-oo-oo" parts as they read the book aloud.

Afterwards, Stephen came to me and said, "I want to write the book." My first thought was a horrified, "*Copy* the book?" but I said nothing. We talked. I suggested he start with one page, knowing that the task would more than challenge his skills. At that time Stephen's own stories consisted of an illustration, his name, and perhaps a few letters—now he wanted to write a book. Then he set to work, coming to ask a question about a particular part of the text and to inform me that he wanted to "write the words": no illustrations. Stephen left the table only for lunch.

Late in the day he read me his finished "book"—a piece of unlined newsprint with each word of Cowley's *The Haunted House* carefully transcribed. He wanted to share it with the class. As he settled in the author's chair and read, his shyness became invisible and the story came alive (Graves and Hansen 1983). We sat quietly and listened. Sensing the importance of Stephen's work, the children applauded when he finished reading, something they seldom do. Stephen had needed to make that book *his*—part of him—so he had "written it," a painstaking process for a child of his abilities. His work was inspiring, but watching him as he worked was even more inspirational.

Because I am a writer, I have begun to look for similarities between my writing processes and the children's. There are many, as we all struggle to find topics, figure out what we want to say, attend to others' responses, and master conventions. But Stephen's experiences as a reader of *The Haunted House* made me look for the first time at my own processes as a reader.

Not long ago a friend lent me a copy of Mary Oliver's book of poetry, *Twelve Moons*. I fell in love with the poem "Sleeping in the Forest." I read it and reread it. I shared it with my friends. I read it aloud to my husband as we sat in the park one afternoon. I "wrote it" into a book where I keep my favorite poems so that it would be mine. Stephen is an emergent reader who uses picture cues, memorization, repetition of text, and some phonetic cues. I am an adult reader with very different strategies, yet we each experienced the same joyful process with a piece of writing that we loved. Stephen reminded me, powerfully, how much a reader can love a book.

Why did Stephen—and the other children in our classroom —love stories? I remembered the first day of school when I had read aloud one of my favorite books, *George and Martha Tons of Fun*, adding the first piece to our literacy puzzle. All year we continued to add pieces—*Curious George, A Ghost Story, A House for Hermit Crab, Mummies Made in Egypt, The Pokey Little Puppy*, and, of course, both of *The Haunted Houses*. And the love affairs with characters, books, and authors began: Miriam and Curious George, Kyle and George and Martha, Stephen and *The Haunted House*, me and Mary Oliver. I understood *what* happened, but I didn't understand *why* until I reexamined my role in the children's learning. I found my answer there, and it startled me like a dousing with cold water.

Stephen and the other children had love stories because I had love stories. When we finally received our copy of *A House for Hermit Crab*, they saw me turn its pages reverently. When I read *George and Martha Tons of Fun*, I laughed out loud. When we couldn't identify the yellow and black winged insect Jilliene found in our classroom, I sent her to the library to find a book on bees. My voice cracked when I read *Badger's Parting Gifts*, and we *all* shouted ". . . it was a terrible, horrible, no good, very bad day" as I read Judith Viorst on school days that were like that.

When we demonstrate a genuine passion for literature to our students, our love stories make theirs inevitable. Without a teacher's own joy in literacy, the literature in our classroom libraries remains just so many words printed on so many pieces of paper, and our classrooms remain just places where children and a teacher congregate each day. But when a reading program is built around a teacher's sharing her passion for books and language, then the classroom can become a literary community, one that young readers can't wait to join.

References

Aliki. 1979. *Mummies Made in Egypt.* New York: Thomas Y. Crowell.

Carle, Eric. 1987. *A House for Hermit Crab.* Saxonville, MA: Picture Book Studio.

Cowley, Joy. 1983a. *Dan, the Flying Man.* Auckland, New Zealand: Shortland.

———. 1983b. *The Haunted House.* Auckland, New Zealand: Shortland.

Graves, Donald, and Jane Hansen. 1983. "The Author's Chair." *Language Arts* 60 (8) (November/December).

Harste, Jerome, Virginia Woodward, and Carolyn Burke. 1984. *Language Stories & Literacy Lessons.* Portsmouth, NH: Heinemann.

Hindley, Judy. 1976. *The Time Traveller Book of Knights and Castles.* London: Usborne.

Lionni, Leo. 1968. *The Biggest House in the World.* New York: Pantheon.

Lowrey, Janette Sebring. 1942. *The Pokey Little Puppy.* Racine, WI: Western.

Marshall, James. 1980. *George and Martha Tons of Fun.* Boston: Houghton Mifflin.

Martin, Bill, Jr. 1970a. *A Ghost Story.* New York: Holt, Rinehart and Winston.

———. 1970b. *The Haunted House.* New York: Holt, Rinehart and Winston.

Oliver, Mary. 1979. *Twelve Moons.* Boston: Little, Brown.

Rey, H. A. 1941. *Curious George.* Boston: Houghton Mifflin.

Varley, Susan. 1984. *Badger's Parting Gifts.* New York: Lothrop, Lee & Shepard.

Viorst, Judith. 1972. *Alexander and the Terrible, Horrible, No Good, Very Bad Day.* New York: Macmillan.

———. 1981. "Learning." In *If I Were in Charge of the World and Other Worries.* New York: Macmillan.

An Author's Perspective
THE ROOM IN WHICH
VAN GOGH LIVED

CYNTHIA RYLANT

I think I make teachers very uncomfortable when I talk about writing. They invite me to their schools, pay me good money to convince their students that writing takes hard work and countless revisions, then I flub it by telling the kids that most of what I write comes quick and clean and nearly perfect the first time I sit down with a pen in hand. I make things worse when I admit that I'd rather go to a movie than write a story, and I blow everything to hell when I reveal that I think writers are born with the word in their blood and the plain truth is not everybody can be a writer.

Not one teacher has ever had the guts to ask me if I think the teaching of writing is a waste of time. After all the seminars and workshops and computer classes teachers have spent their precious free time getting under their belts, they sure aren't going to risk some hotshot writer who rarely *writes* telling them it's been all for naught. No way.

I wish someone had asked. The question would have been a challenge, and I would have been pressed to really take a look at what I think about teachers who believe they can teach children to write creatively. I use "creatively" with great emphasis, for I think anybody can be taught to write in a practical, expository way. But kids are being instructed in the writing of *stories* these days, and that boots them into another room entirely.

It is the room in which Van Gogh lived. And Herman Melville. Edward Hopper and Sylvia Plath. Wolfgang Amadeus Mozart and John Milton. I'd put Jesus Christ and Martin Luther King in the bunch, too, though some might debate whether they were artists.

And that is what we are talking about when we talk about writing stories. We are talking about art, about thinking art and creating art and being an artist every single day of one's life. This is about going fishing as an artist and having relatives over for supper as an artist and walking the aisles of a Woolworth's as an artist. This is not just about flipping up a list of adverbs on the Apple.

And if a teacher in a room full of sixth graders sweating over original stories doesn't understand this, then yes, I say that the teaching of writing in that class is a waste of time. I've met some of these teachers. They don't read, themselves. They don't use words like "beauty" or "art" in their conversations about the teaching of writing. Personally, if I viewed what I do when I sit down with a pen as a "writing process," well, I'd likely be earning a living now making copy for basal readers. Turn anything into a process or a program and you have stepped out of that room Van Gogh and Melville were hanging around in.

I learned how to write from writers. I didn't know any personally. But I read, and two of the people I read wiped me out. Threw me into the Van Gogh room headfirst. Their names are James Agee and William Maxwell. I use their books like food, like sunlight to a plant. Teach me, I say to Agee when I open up *Let Us Now Praise Famous Men*. I randomly turn to a page, I start reading and my breath goes. I cannot possibly, possibly accept mediocrity after this.

Do I think the teaching of creative writing to children is a waste of time? Not if you know how to take their breath away first. Give them standards. Read to them *Ox-Cart Man* and *The Animal Family* and *Birds, Beasts and the Third Thing*. Read these with the same feeling in your throat as when you first see the ocean after driving for hours and hours to get to it. Close the final page of the book with the same reverence you feel as you kiss your sleeping child goodnight. Be quiet. Don't talk the experience to death. Shut up and let these kids feel and think.

Do this a lot. Teach them to be moved and you will be preparing them to move others.

I don't mean to imply that everything they read or write needs to be serious stuff. Humor certainly is art. I think it is far more challenging to write funny than to write serious. Our comics—Charlie Chaplin and Woody Allen on screen, Garrison Keillor and Dorothy Parker in print—these people are so far ahead of the rest of us that it is expecting quite a lot of kids that they understand why humor works and how to use it. But do read to them clever books like *James and the Giant Peach* and *The Stupids Die*, and let them sit with those in silence as well.

I don't think it's a waste of time to teach children to write creatively. This is the one time in their lives when that wonderful right brain, the source of imagination and art, is humming at top speed. It's worth it to see what might happen after a room full of ten-year-old right brains listens to a ton of good literature then hears "Try it" from the front of the room. Take your pencils and try it, kids. No grades. No sweat. Try it like testing a pool of water with your toes. Those of you who want to swim in the Van Gogh pool, go ahead. Those of you who don't, or aren't ready, here: read this great book called *When I Was Young in the Mountains*. It's okay to be only a reader. You can read like an artist.

Those who want to go swimming, to try their hand at making beautiful language, need to be reminded: every writer works differently. Some write best sitting at desks, some write best on front porches. Some write very slowly—one good paragraph can take days—and some write fast and can finish a whole story in one sitting. Some can't write anything but poems and some can't write anything but mystery books that run about 120 pages each. Some write once a day and some write once a year.

And once a teacher reminds them of these things, that teacher has to have the courage to accept the consequences of allowing these children choices about how and what they write and read. Obviously, a lot of control is lost. But teachers who believe creation is possible to control can't teach it. Period. They would do better simply reading aloud to their students all year and believing in the seeds they've planted.

You know what I did yesterday? We had a big storm here in Kent, Ohio, that blew some branches off the trees in my backyard. When everything quieted down, I looked out my kitchen window and decided to go view the damage. I had a cup of tea in my right hand and no shoes on. And I decided to walk through the sopping wet grass of my backyard in my bare feet and drink hot tea. I couldn't remember the last time I'd been barefoot in rain-soaked grass.

Writing is something like that. And if a teacher can understand this without me explaining it, then his or her teaching of writing will not be a waste of time.

It will be an art.

P.S. I wrote this sitting on a beach towel beside a small lake, surrounded by plenty of screaming children, and the hard-rock station was on the loudspeaker. It took me about two hours, no major revisions. This doesn't mean anything—but people are curious.

References

Agee, James. 1988. *Let Us Now Praise Famous Men.* Boston: Houghton Mifflin.

Allard, Harry, and James Marshall. 1981. *The Stupids Die.* Boston: Houghton Mifflin.

Dahl, Roald. 1984. *James and the Giant Peach.* New York: Bantam.

Hall, Donald. 1979. *Ox-Cart Man.* New York: Viking.

Jarrell, Randall. 1965. *The Animal Family.* New York: Pantheon.

Lawrence, D. H. 1982. *Birds, Beasts and the Third Thing: Poems.* New York: Viking.

Rylant, Cynthia. 1982. *When I Was Young in the Mountains.* New York: E. P. Dutton.

———.1987. *This Year's Garden.* New York: Macmillan.

NEBUCHADNEZZAR MEETS DICK AND JANE: A READER'S MEMOIR

GINNY SEABROOK
The Vail-Deane School
Mountainside, New Jersey

*M*y love of reading didn't begin with a book, but I think it did begin with a good story. When I was very small, I lay in the quiet darkness listening to my grandfather's voice. I was near my grandfather, and I was happy and secure as he took me back to a time before I was born and told me stories of growing up on a farm where he played tricks on his sisters. In another time, he said, my gray-haired great aunts were young girls who giggled and teased their brother. They helped in the kitchen, and on Sundays, when the preacher came to dinner, they hid biscuits in their pockets for my grandfather, who ate after the adults had finished. The preacher had a mighty appetite for biscuits.

Once, the boy who was my grandfather went swimming in a pond. He left his clothes on the bank and dropped into the water from the limb of a tree. Aunt Addie found his clothes, waved them and teased him, then ran away with them. Not to be outdone, he climbed out naked and chased her until she dropped the clothes and ran squealing home. I relished the naughtiness of it, I, who had no brothers or sisters, and for a while I was there, too, running through the grass in another time and place. Before I learned to read, I knew that a story could take me away.

My first books were an old set of *The Book of Knowledge* that had belonged to my Uncle Max. My grandmother loved to take naps in the afternoon. She was serious about her naps; she put on a voile nightgown and turned back the bed covers. She tried to coax me to take a nap too, and she thought she could read me to sleep. It hardly ever worked. I would choose about five volumes from the bookcase; I knew their contents by heart, and

I would climb onto the bed and plop the heavy volumes down on the sheets. There were stories and historical accounts and intricate old maps. My favorite stories were historical fiction, though I don't think I really knew they were not true. One was about King Nebuchadnezzar, who went insane and ate grass on his hands and knees amid the hanging gardens of Babylon. There was a thrilling picture of the crazed monarch with his wild hair and eyes. The other favorite was "Childe Roland to the Dark Tower Came." It was scary and sad. The end was vague, but I think the little prince was murdered. I was lucky to live before controlled vocabulary and censored reading for children whose small ears should not be exposed to crazed monarchs and doomed princes. Instead of putting me to sleep, my poor grandmother would nod off and drop the book. When I woke her up to continue the story, she said, "I have read until I'm blue in the face," but she always continued.

These early reading experiences are the happiest memories of my childhood, so it is no wonder that I love to read. I have been reading for a long time and have always thought of it as a happy activity and something that is easy to do. As a teacher, I was troubled when I saw many students who thought they couldn't read because it was too hard. Even more disturbing, I saw students who could read but didn't want to. Reading means so much to me that I didn't want to think that these children would have to live without books. I wanted to understand their attitudes and change their minds.

To be honest, I didn't read anything interesting in school until eighth grade. Dick and Jane couldn't compare to King Nebuchadnezzar. I went to the rest room in English class if the teacher would let me—until we read Longfellow's "Evangeline." It was beautiful, especially "the forest primeval," and I was amazed to know that reading stories and poems could be a part of English class. Maybe English wasn't so bad. In ninth grade we read *Treasure Island* but poked along so slowly that I quickly finished it on my own, and it was then that I learned about secret reading in school. I got a book at the library and hid it inside my textbook or under my desk. I read Agnes DeMille's *Dance to the Piper* in ninth-grade English and sneaked sideways looks at Joe B. Clarkson while the teacher spent weeks on *Treasure Island*. Not much came of the sideways looks, but *Dance to the Piper* was wonderful. I was going to be a famous dancer. I began to read biographies in junior high, and I still read a great deal of nonfiction—books about real people like Gerald Durrell, Beatrix Potter, and others who aren't famous but have done interesting things.

Even though I changed high schools five times in four years and read *Macbeth* in every school, I loved Shakespeare. I read some plays we weren't assigned. I had a wonderful eleventh-grade English teacher in public high school in New York City. Her name was Harriet Haft, and she made us all feel as if we were important people and our class was the high point of her day. The class was a motley group of reading levels and ethnic backgrounds, but Mrs. Haft treated everyone as though she were special, and the class was an island of calm in all our lives. Mrs. Haft once said, "Ladies do not chew gum," and I gave up gum for years. I wanted to be like Mrs. Haft. Mrs. Haft didn't assign book reports.

Most teachers required book reports. It is ironic that I was an avid reader who went almost all of the way through twelve years of school without completing a book assigned for a book report. I *intended* to read the books, but when time grew short, I skipped a chapter, or several chapters, and read just enough to write a credible report. When time was really short, I just read the first and last chapters. I was sure my goose was cooked when one teacher announced that we would be giving oral book reports in front of the class. Disgrace was upon me; I would now pay for all my sins of omission in reading. I walked to the front of the room when it was my turn, wishing that I could fade into thin air. My palms were sweating, and the teacher looked at me and said, "Ginny, tell us how the book ended." I couldn't believe it—I was safe. I had read that chapter. I felt relieved but a little guilty for not having done the assignment.

Why had I felt guilty? I had read all through high school, but none of the books I read had been assigned, and no one knew I had read them. I read Shakespeare, the Readers' Digest condensed versions of *Advise and Consent*, and *The Three Faces of Eve* because my mother got a free copy at her job. I read the poems of Edna St. Vincent Millay, at first because I liked her name and later because I liked her poems. I read the latest naughty novels of Françoise Sagan, and I continued to read nonfiction—the humorists Jean Kerr, Harry Golden, and my favorite autobiography of that time, *Act One* by Moss Hart. But I never wrote book reports on any of them.

I have rarely assigned a written book report to my students. I couldn't bring myself to do it, even when other teachers displayed book reports on the bulletin boards complete with beautifully illustrated jackets. When parents told me that they wished I would make their children read more, that I should assign more book reports, I wondered if I was the only one who had faked reports. Were their minds filled and their lives enriched by the books they had read to report on? I told parents the truth, that I loved reading except when I had to read for a book report, and I couldn't do that to my students. They didn't press me again immediately. I think they just wanted their children to read more and were searching for answers. I was supposed to be the expert, but I didn't know how to get students to read more, either. Why did we have to *make* them read? I had always thought of reading as a stolen delight.

In college, my professors seemed to think that reading literature allowed us into a private club where ordinary mortals could not tread. I wanted to be in the club. I had little time for pleasure reading during those years, since I was reading several hours a day for my courses. The reading did make me think, and I became more interested in poetry during college. I took a course in Romantic poets and read Keats and Shelley and Wordsworth, but a professor of freshman English influenced me even more.

I was having difficulty choosing a topic to research. In a conference in his office, the professor gave me a volume of e. e. cummings' poems and asked me to read one out loud. He might as well have asked me to sing in Russian. Here was a strange-looking poem without capitals and punctuation. I wondered if the professor was playing some kind of joke on me, but he seemed serious. I could make nothing of the poem, and I guess he realized that he had expected too much of me. He then recommended Robert Frost, whom I researched, read, and re-read for many years.

But I couldn't let go of e. e. cummings. I didn't like not understanding something, and I went to the bookstore and bought a book of his poems and gave myself headaches trying to puzzle them out. It was a challenge. I didn't like to think that the poet would write poems I couldn't understand; I *would* unravel the meaning. Finally I gave up and put the poems away. It was not until sometime later, when I no longer regarded cummings as a personal adversary, that his poetry began to get through to me. When I didn't try, I got it—at least some of it. I hadn't yet learned that every time I read a poem I see it a little differently.

I realized that it was possible to try too hard. I suppose when I finally got it, I was not reading with the attitude that I had to play a game with the poet to get at his secret meaning.

I didn't translate this experience very well in my teaching. For years, I hated teaching poetry because I liked poems and the students didn't. I dreaded the poetry unit because I knew I would fail again. I was still trying to teach the secret meanings. I tried so hard to tell them what I saw, never realizing that the poem could not mean exactly the same thing to them. Only in the past year have I had success teaching poetry. The change came when I attended some workshops that taught poetry through reading it aloud. I tried that in class, just reading and letting my students read. We concentrated on how the poem sounded and forgot about what it might mean. The students relaxed and began to like the poems we read over and over. They began to *listen* to the words and think about what they meant. And I began to realize that it was fine if students just got a little bit, as I had done with e. e. cummings.

I also read classics in college. Stendhal's *The Red and the Black* and the Russian novel *Crime and Punishment* made only a slight impression on me. I remember that *Moby Dick* had seven layers of meaning and lots of incredibly tedious chapters on the finer points of whaling. My serious interest in whales and other marine mammals did not begin with Moby. It seems to be one of those badges that English majors wear; colleges should print T-shirts with the logo "This sophomore survived *Moby Dick*."

It was after I was married that I read most of the classics that I love and return to like old friends. Jane Austen tops the list. I have read all of her novels many times; I read *Emma* again last spring. *Pride and Prejudice* was a catchy title; I had heard of it in high school. I checked it out of the library several times and tried to read it. It seemed like a book I ought to read. I didn't understand it; I didn't see the humor in it. I would read a little and wonder why it was a great book and take it back. One day after I was out of college, I picked it up and laughed my way through the first chapter. Why had I never laughed at Mrs. Bennet's poor nerves? I knew this family; some of the Bennets were my relatives too. It was, of course, the same book I had tried before, but I was a different person—perhaps a better reader, older, wiser, more relaxed. When I was in high school, it never occurred to me that a great book could be funny. This book was very funny; the people were real. Some years later when we went to Derbyshire, I felt that I might meet Mr. Darcy on the street, and I would know him right away.

I also read *Wuthering Heights* and then *Jane Eyre*. I turned the pages and wept on the book in my bedroom there in Newark. My husband laughed at me and said it was an English soap opera. I didn't care; I just kept reading and weeping. In college I read books that the professors assigned, wrote critical papers, took essay tests. But I have not returned to Stendhal, nor have I reread *Crime and Punishment*. The classics that I read as an assignment have not become part of me.

The classics that I really love are the ones I read when I was older and out of school. I seldom tried to teach classics because it would be very sad if my students felt forced to read Jane Austen if they couldn't see the humor or didn't understand *Jane Eyre* well enough to cry. I often think of *To Kill a Mockingbird* and Atticus Finch's words about getting in someone else's shoes and walking around in order to understand that person. When I read classics in school, I knew what the words meant, but I didn't have enough experience with being alive to understand the people. I couldn't walk around in their shoes. I am afraid that if a teacher had made me read those books, I would have developed an unfortunate distaste for them and would not have picked them up again years later when I could appreciate the characters.

My own experience tells me that we need not assume that if the classics aren't assigned, they won't be read. I read them after I was an adult, and I still read them. If we can develop a love of books in our students, they will develop their own tastes and I think will choose many classics on their own. Why do we think our students are any less likely to read them than we are? Do English teachers read only classics? I doubt it. In between Jane Austen and Dickens I read Agatha Christie and Elspeth Huxley. I read Lucy Calkins and Richard Wilbur and Donald Graves. I haven't read all of the classics. I have not read *Silas Marner*. (I may be the only English teacher in America who has not read *Silas Marner*. All the high schools I went to were doing *Macbeth*.)

When my son and daughter were born, I enjoyed reading to them as much as I enjoyed having my grandmother read to me, and I think they helped me develop a genuine interest in adolescent literature. They introduced me to C. S. Lewis and Roald Dahl, and I continued to read Madeline L'Engle after Jack and Susie had outgrown her. These books were a whole new source of pleasure. I have read many of the books that I buy for my classroom and recommend to students. I read them because they are good stories. I really enjoy the novels of Katherine Paterson, Mildred Taylor, Virginia Hamilton, and Cynthia Voigt.

I don't know why it took me so long to learn that I can help children become readers. I had many of the right questions, but not enough answers. Reading came to my rescue. When I began to do more professional reading, I discovered that others had the answers to the questions on my mind. I got new ideas about how students read from Frank Smith (1985). Lucy Calkins (1986) and Donald Graves (1983) said that I have to learn from my students: a novel idea. Did my students have something to teach me? Did my own experience as a student have something to teach me?

As I thought, I came to realize that time was important. Children don't have much time. They go to tennis lessons, baseball practice, piano and dance lessons; they watch their favorite TV shows, go to Catechism and Hebrew School. It made me weary just thinking of all the things they had to do after school. They seldom had those wonderful quiet afternoons I remember spending on the front porch when I was their age. That slower-moving life is as far in the past as my grandfather's skinny dipping days were to me. How could I give my students time when I had no control over their after-school activities?

It was not until I read Atwell's *In the Middle* (1987) that I began to think of allowing students time to read in class. I could give them in school something that I had had outside of school. Letting students read during class was an uncomfortable idea to me. Perhaps because I thought reading was fun, I felt guilty about spending class time on it. I thought I should be "doing something." I thought students should be "working."

Last year I gave my students time to read, and I let them choose their own books. I wasn't sure what would happen. I was surprised when they were willing to sit and read for an entire class period, and I didn't mind that they clearly preferred reading to listening to me. They were reading, and they liked it. Instead of talking, I read with them. In the past I had told them about books I had read, but this was the first time they had seen me read. In my experience, reading quietly was not what teachers were supposed to do in class. Even after the reading periods were a success, it took time for me to feel comfortable as, book in hand, I stepped out of my role as one who tells students what to do and assumed the place of a reader among readers. I became one who shows students how to do something that I enjoy. I was surprised to find that my students and I had more in common than I had imagined. They and I could lose ourselves in a good story, and we thought about what we read. We had literary discussions instead of question-and-answer sessions, and I learned from what my students said.

Once I had thought that I already knew all there was to know about teaching English. I thought I knew what students needed to learn, and I decided when they would learn it. I call it the Brussels sprout method of teaching. I was the well-meaning mom who thought Brussels sprouts were good for her children, and I was determined to feed them sprouts whether they wanted them or not. I haven't dumped the Brussels sprouts, but I have put them on the table with a lot of other things. And the students can eat what they like. Some eat Brussels sprouts.

I want my students to be skillful and voracious readers. I grew up reading and loving books. I want to pass on my love of reading, my independence as a learner. I want my students to step outside of themselves and try on other lives, the lives of the people they meet in books. I am prepared to be surprised by what students choose and what they know. And I feel that I am more important as a teacher than I have ever been. I listen to their comments and I decide when to dive in and teach them something—not from teachers' manuals but something from my store of knowledge about literature and life that will extend their own ideas.

I am giving students the gift of their own thoughts, the gift of other times and other places. I am letting the storytellers like my grandfather work their ancient magic.

References

Atwell, Nancie. 1987. *In the Middle: Writing, Reading, and Learning with Adolescents*. Portsmouth, NH: Boynton/Cook.

Austen, Jane. 1966. *Emma*. New York: Washington Square.

———. 1970. *Pride and Prejudice*. New York: Washington Square.

Brontë, Charlotte. 1976. *Jane Eyre*. London: Purnell.

Brontë, Emily. 1942. *Wuthering Heights*. New York: Dodd, Mead.

Calkins, Lucy McCormick. 1986. *The Art of Teaching Writing*. Portsmouth, NH: Heinemann.

Drury, Allen. 1959. *Advise and Consent*. New York: Doubleday.

DeMille, Agnes. 1951. *Dance to the Piper*, Series in Dance. New York: Da Capo.

Dostoyevesky, Fyodor. 1950. *Crime and Punishment*. New York: The Modern Library.

Graves, Donald H. 1983. *Writing: Teachers & Children at Work.* Portsmouth, NH: Heinemann.

Hart, Moss. 1959. *Act One.* New York: Random House.

Lee, Harper. 1960. *To Kill a Mockingbird.* Philadelphia: Lippincott.

Longfellow, Henry W. 1975. "Evangeline." In *The Poetical Works of Longfellow.* Boston: Houghton Mifflin.

Melville, Herman. 1950. *Moby Dick.* New York: Random House.

Shakespeare, William. 1956. *Macbeth.* New York: Penguin.

Smith, Frank. 1985. *Reading Without Nonsense.* New York: Teachers College.

Stendhal. 1949. *The Red and the Black.* Garden City, NY: The Literary Guild of America.

Stevenson, Robert Louis. 1981. *Treasure Island.* New York: Bantam.

Thigpen, Corbutt H., and Hervey M. Cleckley. 1957. *The Three Faces of Eve.* Kingsport, TN: Kingsport.

THE SILENCES
BETWEEN THE LEAVES

MARNI SCHWARTZ
Niskayuna Middle School
Schenectady, New York

I had to learn it. My brother Jimmy said, "If you want to be in drama club, Marni, you take what Mr. Quirk assigns."

"But a choral reading?" I whined. It just didn't seem fair. I thought drama club meant *plays*. Who wanted to learn some dumb old ballad about a kid going to a fiddling contest?

But learn it I did. Back in ninth grade Mr. Quirk hooked me on a story that has become both teacher and friend. By now I've told Stephen Vincent Benét's "The Mountain Whippoorwill" hundreds of times. Though the words remain the same, the story's meaning continues to change—sometimes subtly, sometimes dramatically. I can find a strange newness in it when I tell it to the road on long drives to unknown cities. It's different when shared with wide-eyed first graders or memory-soaked senior citizens. My middle schoolers bring something else to it, as do my colleagues. Aside from the audience, *I* keep bringing new issues to the tale. It is my story. With a little help from Mr. Quirk it found me that first year in high school. Now, in every telling, I discover in it something I didn't know before (or had forgotten) about my fears or my joys or how I fit myself to the world.

In school, children don't often get the chance to reread, let alone retell, one story over and over: so much good literature and so little time. I know wide reading offers children the infinite possibilities of language, that it allows them to compare character types, themes, story structures, and authors' styles. Yet my experiences in storytelling, especially with "Whippoorwill," have taught me the importance of not only allowing but *encouraging*

31

children to return regularly to one or perhaps a few key stories they can love and cherish all their lives.

John Moffitt writes about the necessity of spending time with something you claim to know.

**To Look
at
Any Thing**

To look at any thing,
If you would know that thing,
You must look at it long:
To look at this green and say
"I have seen spring in these
Woods," will not do—you must
Be the thing you see:
You must be the dark snakes of
Stems and ferny plumes of leaves,
You must enter in
To the small silences between
The leaves,
You must take your time
And touch the very peace
They issue from.

Storytelling has allowed me and my students to "be the dark snakes of stems and ferny plumes of leaves." We can step inside the skins of the villains we abhor and the heroes we admire. We can win the prize or escape the danger again and again, and in doing so come to know prizes and dangers in new and sometimes startling ways.

Each year my students reteach me the value of storytelling as a way to connect to literature and to know themselves. I haven't yet followed a student's companionship with one tale over time, though I've seen glimpses of kids holding tightly to stories. In tracing my attachment to "Whippoorwill" and sharing what I learn with students, I hope that I might induce them to think about the stories that have been important to them and consider that holding on to a story over a lifetime will teach them a lot about themselves. I also hope that I might entice other teachers to storytell the tales or excerpts of the longer works they love and invite their students to "touch the very peace" of a story through telling.

After ninth grade, I didn't reconnect with the Benét piece until I unearthed it from my mother's files for an undergraduate

English methods course. My oral expression lesson plan, basically an imitation of Mr. Quirk's coaching, received an A, but trying the choral telling with inner-city high school kids is what truly endeared me to the poem. My students fell for the young fiddler and his mountain talk just the way my friends and I had back in drama club. As a student I had shone in rehearsed readings; in spontaneous readings I got caught between trying to use expression *and* comprehend. As a student teacher, I hoped to offer my charges the taste of the success I'd had performing the choral reading with friends. Out came Mr. Quirk's dark voices/ light voices script, which my mother had saved with other high school mementos. I just retyped and mimeographed it. The script called for a few solo lines, which many wanted to claim. We did the reading over and over until everyone who wanted a solo part got one. I was surprised by how different the work sounded each time. The individual personalities enlivened the solos, and each reading shaded the darks and lights of the poem. But I was yet to see how a retelling could *mean* something different as well.

I awoke to the work's ability to change in meaning when it evolved in my mind's eye from poem to story. I used that lesson plan almost every year of my early teaching, it was so much fun. Then, during my first visit to a support group for storytellers, I was encouraged to "just tell the story."

"But it's a poem!" I countered. "I don't have a copy with me."

"Just tell it like a story," the leader of the group repeated. "If you fall into the rhythms of the poem, fine. If you're stuck for words, just keep telling what happened."

I began to picture the characters in my mind, and I began to know them. Previously, I had described "Big Tom Sargent," "Little Jimmy Weezer," "Old Dan Wheeling," and "the ruck of the bob-tailed fiddlers," but I hadn't really seen them. Once the characters became images, the whole story began to change for me. I've since seen this phenomenon with my student storytellers. When they let go of the text and step into the images of a tale or poem, they cast a spell over listeners, inviting the audience inside the world of the story.

Once I crawled inside "Whippoorwill," I started to identify with the narrator in new ways. He is a kid who grows up in the mountains where "it's lonesome all the time." He says, "Never knew my pappy," "Never had a mammy to teach me pretty-please," "Never had a brother ner a whole pair of pants," and "never raised a pet." Now, that wording does not exactly describe my childhood. I lived in a house on a busy main street with five siblings, various dogs (once briefly a turtle and a rooster), two parents (both teachers), and two grandparents; the other two grandparents lived five minutes away by car. Yet in a house like that one could feel lonesome. Everyone was bustling, doing chores or hiding to escape them, and I remember feeling alone with my fantasies. In those days I told myself stories. Years later, it was like discarding a set of blinders to discover that "Up in the mountains, it's lonesome for a child" were words about me, not just a hillbilly fiddler.

In the story, Benét uses both italics and parentheses when the speaker whispers to his fiddle. The instrument is the only physical companion he has brought with him from the hills. "(*Listen, little whippoorwill yuh better bug yore eyes!*)" But he's also brought his pride. He announces to the crowd, "Anyone that licks me— well, he's got to fiddle hard!" He carries as well "the sound of the squirrel in the pine" and echoes of "the earth a breathin' through the long nighttime" to help him play. Slowly, these phrases began to trigger the sound symbols I carry from childhood into tests of confidence. I often go where "kingpin" storytellers (and award-winning teachers and prolific writers) go and feel myself trembling in their midst. Then I too have to recall the sound of my mother singing or perhaps the steady ticking of our livingroom clock or the hiss of traffic on West First Street, and I have to tell myself, "Bug yore eyes."

"The Mountain Whippoorwill" is really a story of confidence. Early in the poem, the young fiddler appears rather cocky to the "jedges an' the rest" at the Essex County Fair. He plunks a silver dollar in front of them and dares anyone to beat him. But slowly, as each skilled fiddler plays, the boy's confidence wanes. He says of Old Dan Wheeling,

> When he was finished, the crowd cut loose,
> (*Whippoorwill, they's rain on yore breast.*)
> An' I sat there wonderin' "What's the use?"
> (*Whippoorwill, fly home to yore nest.*)

Saying those lines, I'm suddenly a young, green schoolteacher who almost turned and fled her first tough eighth grade. I'm the little girl who silently dreaded the out-of-town swimming and diving meets my father sneaked us into because "the competition'll be good for you." I'm the lonely exchange student tortured by my Malaysian sister's three-week silent treatment. Yet each time those lines are followed by:

But I stood up pert an' I took my bow,
An' my fiddle went to my shoulder, so.

An'—they wasn't no crowd to get me fazed—
But I was alone where I was raised.

Those lines make me stronger and surer everytime I speak them.
They teach me that confidence won't fail me.

The boy then acknowledges just how unique his own fiddling is.

They've fiddled the rose, an' they've fiddled the thorn,
But they haven't fiddled the mountain-corn.

They've fiddled sinful an' fiddled moral,
But they haven't fiddled the breshwood-laurel.

They've fiddled loud, an' they've fiddled still,
But they haven't fiddled the whippoorwill.

I tell this story for those lines mostly. I want my students to
honor their uniqueness. It's not always easy to know, let alone
express, how individual students are talented, what special contribution they alone have to make to the world. "I'm not any
good at anything," some tell me in September. Many associate
achievement with sports or good grades, encouraged by our
society's fixation with competition and winning. (Ironically, some
schools introduce storytelling through contests, but I discourage
that everywhere I go. A story festival can be just as breathtaking.)
Talent comes in many flavors. I remind both my students and
myself of that each time I say, "But they haven't fiddled the
whippoorwill."

It's only recently, through retelling this poem, that I've begun
to see how the stress of competition was an intricate part of my
childhood. "Them that got the mostest claps'd win the bestest
prize," the narrator claims. I knew that "Whippoorwill" was the
story of a contest, but one day the telling changed in a major
way, and I tripped over some unexpected insights about my
formative years. Being born third, I developed a natural rivalry
with my two older siblings, trying to do whatever they could do.
The fact that they were boys made it worse.

Like my brothers, I was encouraged to be competitive. I remember talent contests, essay contests, costume contests, awards
for best this and best that throughout my childhood. It all made
me uneasy: the pressure not to choke, the constant measuring
of one kid's talent against another's, the glaring spotlights (for

the winners), and the shadows never dark enough to hide a loser's shame. I competed willingly then and still find the competitor alive in me today, but my reflections on "Whippoorwill" have awakened me to the power that winning and losing held over me as a child.

As a result, the first hundred times or so I told "The Mountain Whippoorwill" I told it sad. Listeners often cried near the end when it seems the young fiddler has lost.

> They wasn't a sound when I stopped bowin'
> (*Whippoorwill, yuh can sing no more.*)
> An' I thought, "I've fiddled all night an' lost.
> Yo're a good hill-billy, but yuh've been bossed."

My voice would crack, not for dramatic effect, but because inside I cried for this child who has given every ounce of his talent and courage and who believes he has lost. The insight, naturally, is that I was crying for myself, for the little girl who was coaxed onto stage, onto the diving board, into rivalry as a way of living.

One day, I found myself telling the story funny. I said the same words but with a kind of Gomer Pyle guffaw. At first, this puzzled me. Then I realized I'd mourned the little girl enough and let the sadness go. The ending—when the young fiddler goes "to congratulate old man Dan," but instead "he put his fiddle into my han'-/ An' then the noise of the crowd began"— is just as powerful whether I go in laughing or crying. I like it better laughing, though some in the audience still cry. They bring who they are or once were to the tale. I've also discovered my new insight humbles me as a parent—one who drives a child to soccer and baseball games, swimming meets, piano recitals, and essay contest readings. Where would we be without hindsight?

Other discoveries about the story have surprised and pleased me. There is no gender given to the narrator except in the poem's subtitle: "Or, How Hill-Billy Jim Won the Great Fiddlers' Prize." Mr. Quirk's copy didn't show that, so I've never included it in my telling. I assumed the fiddler was a boy—never occurred to me in high school that a girl would compete with "smarty" men fiddlers. But times change. Once I was talking with kids about the poem's ending. It comes very fast and can be confusing for young listeners the first time they hear it. I asked, "Why might the crowd have stayed silent when the boy 'stopped bowin' '?" A little girl blurted out, "The boy?! You mean it was a boy?" I smiled. Of course, the fiddler should be a girl for girl readers.

I wish it could have been for me earlier, but today the image of the fiddler in my mind is somehow sexless. Now, I simply say "fiddler" if I ask my listeners questions.

Some insights into a literary work take a longer time to surface. In this poem the fiddling of each character is described in a string of images. Many are country images. Big Tom Sargent "could fiddle all the bugs off a sweet-potatoe vine" or "fiddle down a possum from a mile-high tree." In a long stanza near the end of the poem, the narrator describes his own fiddling through the many images he associates with growing up in the mountains. Saying these wonderful phrases, especially reciting this long stanza the way a "red-hot" fiddler might play, is one of the joys of telling the poem. Many of these are country expressions as well.

> Swing yore partners-up an' down the middle!
> Sashay now-oh, listen to that fiddle!
> Flapjacks flippin' on a red-hot griddle,

Later in the stanza we hear,

> Rabbit in the pea-patch, possum in the pot,
> Try an' stop my fiddle, now my fiddle's gettin' hot!

Several of the images are from Bible stories. I'd rattled off such phrases as "Jonah sittin' on a hickory-bough, / Up jumps a whale—an' where's yore prophet now?" countless times and never recognized that the music of both the young fiddler and the king-pin fiddler, the two most admired by the crowd, was dominated by biblical allusion. Old Dan Wheeling "fiddled a most almighty tune," "fiddled salvation everywhere," and "ended fiddlin' like a host." The young fiddler countered with "Fire on the mountains—snakes in the grass. / Satan's here a-bilin'—oh, Lordy, let him pass!" There are references to the "burnin' bush," "the stable door," and "the old Red Sea." Like "flapjacks" and "pea patches," these images were simply part of life for most Southern mountain folk. As an upstate New York teenager reciting the words with my friends in drama club, I never made that connection of a people to their religious heritage. I laugh to think how many times as a teacher of literature—you know, the one who's supposed to have all the answers—I said those words and still didn't get that connection. But over all those years I was getting other things. I'm not sure why, but recently the Bible stories I heard as a child—of Moses as a foundling, of young David before the giant, of Jesus lingering in the temple when his parents had gone—started coming back to me as do the fiddler's to him. Those in my audience must be hearing the telling differently too. Someone recently commented about the Biblical aspect of the poem, "You couldn't tell that poem in my church without everyone joining in." I smiled to think of the change that would make in the telling!

While drafting this article, I was shocked by yet another discovery about the poem. I'd misplaced my copy of the original dog-eared script from Mr. Quirk so I headed to the library. The minute I opened the thick collection of Benét's works I spotted words I'd never seen before. Two whole stanzas plus several refrain lines of "Oh, hell's broke loose in Georgia" were missing from my version of the fast-moving fiddling section near the end. I share them here with delight:

> Oh, Georgia booze is mighty fine booze,
> The best yuh ever poured yuh,
> But it eats the soles right offen yore shoes,
> For Hell's broke loose in Georgia.
>
> My mother was a whippoorwill pert,
> My father, he was lazy,
> But I'm Hell broke loose in a new store shirt
> To fiddle all Georgia crazy.

I was stunned, but I laughed to think that whoever basalized the version I grew up with (and Mr. Quirk and I unwittingly handed down to so many others) had a toleration for the host of heaven but not the powers of hell. I must admit the fiddling scene evokes a whole new set of images now. So be it.

Though it has taken me years to discover these personal interpretations of the poem, doing so has made me believe I can now help students dig deeper into the literature they encounter. I can invite students inside "the small silences between the leaves" of poems, folktales, short stories, and novels, or even of their own original literature, through storytelling. Not every piece can be storytold, but through drama, art, music, or dance students might interpret and reinterpret a work—and in the end know themselves and the literature a little better. Children will come to their own meanings of literature if we encourage them, as Moffitt's poem urges, to take their time.

We just never know what we might get started. Thanks, Mr. Quirk.

Bill Quirk taught English and drama from 1958 to 1985 in Fulton, New York.

References

Benét, Stephen Vincent. 1942. "The Mountain Whippoorwill." In *The Selected Works of Stephen Vincent Benét.* New York: Holt, Rinehart and Winston.

Moffitt, John. 1961. "To Look at Any Thing." In *The Living Seed.* New York: Harcourt, Brace & World.

RESPONDING
TO THE CALL

KATHY MATTHEWS
George B. White School
Deerfield, New Hampshire

*T*he gods and goddesses, heroes and heroines of Ancient
Greece hovered in clusters around the base of Mount Olympus,
talking, laughing, and admiring each others' clothes. Hercules,
wrapped in his lion's skin, boasted with Theseus about their
famous deeds. Aphrodite admired Artemis's bow, while Medea
chatted enthusiastically with Hera. Athena showed Perseus how
she had secured Medusa's head to her aegis, and Persephone
and Demeter giggled and whispered each time Hades sauntered
by. Hermes, all silver and fleet of foot, slipped in and out of
conversations, dropping jokes and comments. Then Iris, God-
dess of the Rainbow and messenger to Queen Hera, quietly
announced that it was time for the festival to begin. Talk softened
to a murmur as the immortal ones arranged themselves for their
descent to the world of the mortals and a festival in their honor.

A scene from a Greek myth? It could have been. In reality it
was one moment from my third graders' culminating celebration
of their study of the culture and mythology of Ancient Greece.
Mount Olympus was a five-foot-tall, painted cardboard pyramid
that stood in the center of our classroom. It crowned a table-
sized diorama of Poseidon's Kingdom, Earth, and Hades—the
components of the Greeks' world. The gods and goddesses, of
course, were the children and I, costumed as our favorite mythological characters. The festival was an opportunity to share our
experiences and projects with the children's families and the
members of our community.

In our "amphitheater" that evening, two groups of children
performed their own versions of the classic tales of Perseus and

Persephone, using elaborate puppets that they had made. Guests wandered through exhibits of the children's work, admiring the results of weeks of problem-solving and labor: Aaron's scale model of the Parthenon, Debbie's version of the Minotaur's maze, the wings Mike had built so that he could fly like Icarus, Jenny's lifelike Pegasus perched for flight, embroidered tapestries of Athena, Prometheus, and Aphrodite, the twelve dioramas Chad and Amber sculpted in plasticene to symbolize the labors of Hercules, Matt and Nate's relief map of Ancient Greece, and our clay pots painted with classic Greek designs and seeded with Greek herbs. The guests talked with the children about their work, read the reports they had written, and feasted on traditional Greek fare including that classic bacchanalian drink—grape juice.

In our school, where there are no basals and curriculum is created by the teachers, third graders traditionally study the global community and the effects that contrasting climates have on the development of differing cultures. Teachers are free to interpret the curriculum and these global concepts in any way we choose. When my second-grade class and I moved to third grade this past year, I decided to focus on ancient civilizations and to use mythology as a unifying theme.

My original plan was to begin briefly with prehistoric cultures, move to the Greeks and Romans, then study Nordic culture, ending with the Celts, Medieval life, and the legend of King Arthur, the point in history when ancient religions and Christianity seem to have merged. But the children's intense enthusiasm changed my plans, and within the first two weeks of school I had set my original schedule aside. Rather than spending several weeks on the life and mythologies of prehistoric cultures and Ancient Greece, we ended up focusing on these areas for the first six months of the school year and then moved on to the Norsemen and Celts.

There were several reasons that I chose to use mythology as a unifying theme, the most important being the recent impact that mythology has had on my own life. My only formal experience with myths was in ninth grade, when we did a three-week unit on the Greeks and Romans. The myths were presented as entertaining stories, totally devoid of the richness of their original contexts. I enjoyed the unit, but since I was taught to see myths only as amusing reflections of primitive thought, rather than the expressions of human experience that they truly are, the myths had little impact on my life. Over the years I missed the significance in the metaphors that myths have provided for the literature, politics, science, math, poetry, philosophy, and education I read and studied. Two years ago that changed when a friend introduced me to the lucid, poetic works of Joseph Campbell. She warned that I was about to fall into Alice's rabbit hole. She was right. Myths are compelling, and I have been pulled deeper and deeper into their meanings ever since. Because myths magnify life and take our vision beyond the realm of our own immediate existence, I felt connected to some great truth I had never known was missing. Mythology is a key to our culture, but if no one ever helps us to discover it, we can spend our lives never making the connection. I didn't want this to happen to the children I teach.

Mythology has played an important part in the way children have been taught since the beginning of time; in fact, for thousands of years, it was the only way they were taught. Our culture, though, leached away the power of myths and reduced them to mere "units of study" in junior high and high school. It is usually assumed that younger children are too immature to comprehend myths, yet I think there are amazing parallels between the thinking of third graders and the thinking of the ancients. Third graders teeter on the cusp between reality and fantasy. They know that reindeer can't fly but believe in Santa Claus. They know the moon is Earth's satellite, a sphere of dust and craters devoid of life, yet maintain that the moon, of its own volition, follows them wherever they go. They laugh to think that the Greeks actually believed Cronus ate his children and spit them out alive, yet they still revel in the tale of Little Red Riding Hood. Third graders have the advantage of science and technology to help them understand the world but, in many ways, their understanding is still as embryonic and imaginative as that of our distant ancestors.

A third reason that I decided to choose mythology as a theme is its significance to the ancient civilizations as something greater than a religion. Mythology was their vision of their world; as such, it governed their thinking, politics, warfare, art, and daily chores. What better vehicle for comprehending the essence of these civilizations than through the stories around which their entire culture revolved?

We began our study by looking back in time at our own lives to get a sense of how history develops. Borrowing an idea from Linda Rief, an eighth-grade teacher in Durham, New Hampshire, I had the children construct personal time lines based on the most significant positive and negative events for each year of their lives. In writing about these memories, interviewing their parents, and searching through personal artifacts, the children had an opportunity to experience what it is like to construct history and to write about it.

From this point we began to look at prehistoric cultures, to see how these evolved over time into distinct civilizations. My original intention was to spend no more than a week and a half on this topic, but the children's enthusiasm quickly led us down some wondrous and unexpected paths. Suddenly, instead of a brief overview of prehistory, we were studying human anatomy and physiology, caves and spelunking, prehistoric art, tools and machines, prey-predator relationships, and archaeology. We covered our four-by-eight-foot classroom loft with paper and painted it to look like a deep, dark cave. Its interior was quickly graced with the children's paintings of their "hunts" and the mythical animals they created in their dramatic play, as well as a skeleton borrowed from the junior high. They spent hours poring through reference books, learning the names of bones, and comparing the present shape of humans to their ancestors.

We visited America's Stonehenge, a prehistoric site in southern New Hampshire where children were able to crawl in and out of caves, try their hand at being an oracle, and shudder at the image of blood collecting in the deep grooves of the sacrificial table. We read books about archaeology and conducted an archeological dig of our own in the foundation of an old barn that my husband and I had torn down. With field notebooks in hand, teams of children marked out grids, excavated, and recorded their findings. The hit of the day was a well-preserved chicken. For several days the archeological teams worked to clean, sort, and classify their artifacts. The children developed their own ways of classifying and recording their information and experienced yet another form of thinking and another function of written language.

Our study of Greece began at the beginning with stories about how the world was shaped from Chaos, how the Titans were overthrown, and how Zeus came to rule the world. Each morning I focused on one mythological character. Using resources such as *Gods, Men, and Monsters from Greek Myths* and *D'Aulaire's Book of Greek Myths*, I shared myths that pertained to the character's birth, family relationships, and famous deeds and adventures. During the same session we also studied the color plates in art and history books to see how the Greeks (and subsequent artists) portrayed the character in their art, architecture, and daily lives.

Our afternoon meetings always began with lengthier, chapter-book read-alouds—*Jason and the Argonauts, The Deadly Power* of *Medusa, Theseus and the Minotaur, The Children's Homer,* and *The Odyssey*—that, in turn, became independent reading choices for the children.

Our room was filled with books about Ancient Greece and its mythology. We borrowed from the school library, the university library, my personal collection, and the collections of parents and staff members. The books ranged from technical architecture texts to picture books to "I Can Read" adaptations of familiar Greek tales to a children's book written in Greek. The books were in constant use throughout the entire day. Children read and reread their favorite stories, shared their favorite myths with each other, and continuously consulted the material as they conducted research for their projects and writing.

The literature provided opportunities to explore a wide range of experiences. These weren't just enjoyable, isolated activities; rather, they were integrated and intertwined experiences that were generated one from another. Sometimes children worked alone on independent projects of their choice, such as creating the Minotaur's maze or a scale model of the Parthenon. Generally, though, children worked in small collaborative groups that were responsible for separate projects like the construction of a Trojan horse or a particular component of a larger class project like the epic murals of the Argonauts and Odysseus.

We studied geometry, astronomy, astrology, the origins of machines, and ancient forms of measurement. We turned our loft into the Parthenon, complete with reliefs and friezes. We constructed a giant model of the Trojan horse. We covered the walls of our classroom and hall with murals of the adventures of Jason and his Argonauts and the tragic siege of Troy. Life-size gods and goddesses hung on our walls next to giant paintings of mythical beasts. Constellations bearing mythical names covered the ceiling tiles. We visited the Greek collection at the Boston Museum of Fine Arts and spent time sketching these magnificent works of art. We grew pots of herbs associated with Greek myths and made masks for Greek tragedies and dramas. As Greek astrologers the children worked on horoscopes, created their own constellations, and wrote myths to explain their origins.

Like Homer and other great poets before them, my students also created poems and songs and plays and stories to represent their own versions of ancient myths. The following piece is an excerpt from a song that was begun by Matt and finished by the class. To the tune of "Frère Jacques":

Medusa

Medusa, Medusa
was a Gorgon, was a Gorgon,
with a head of snakes, with a head of snakes
fangs and claws, fangs and claws.

King Polydictes, King Polydictes,
told young Perseus, told young Perseus,
"Cut Medusa's head off. Cut Medusa's head off,
and bring it back. Bring it back."

Poor Perseus, poor Perseus,
didn't know what to do, didn't know what to do.
Along came Athena, along came Athena,
and Hermes, too. Hermes, too. . . .

The song continues for many verses to describe the entire epic of Perseus slaying Medusa and saving Andromeda, and was only one of many ways that children innovated on text and ideas in order to create their own meanings from the myths.

Two important things happened as a result of embracing mythology as a unifying theme to our year. First, we learned more about the universality of stories and human experience. And second, we all gained greater access to the deeper meanings of our own culture.

Myths are metaphors for universal human experiences (Campbell 1969). The metaphors are most commonly expressed in archetypes such as creation, resurrection, the hero's quest, the loss of innocence, or the theft of fire, and in such motifs as the sun, the moon, shapes, numbers, snakes, and owls, to name a few (Stillman 1985). The children learned to recognize these archetypes and motifs in the individual cultures they studied as well as across all cultures.

Of even greater importance, they began to recognize mythological prototypes in the stories they created and in the literature they read every day—to contemplate themes and motifs in favorite books like *The Secret Garden*. They explored the idea that Colin, like Heracles and Jason before him, had to be courageous and struggle hard to get what he wanted. They discussed how the robin leading Mary to the key was like the ants helping Psyche sort the grain. They compared Dickon's magical way with animals to Orpheus' power to subdue the wildest beasts with his music. Again and again, I was surprised and delighted by the depth and clarity of their understanding.

Another wonderful thing that occurred was that the children began to recognize the pervasive influence of Greek civilization and classical mythology on our own culture. Everyday words, phrases, symbols, and concepts suddenly took on new meaning. Children brought in newspaper and magazine clippings that advertised cars named Taurus and Mercury and scouring cleaners called Ajax. They learned why a book of maps was called an atlas, where the names of the weekdays came from, and how English words could be related by using Greek roots such as -*graph*. Expressions such as "the face that launched a thousand ships" and "undertaking an odyssey" suddenly made sense. They learned that the satellites of planets like Jupiter could be more easily remembered by recalling mythological associations. They learned the origin of names for minerals like mercury, uranium, and plutonium, plants like iris and narcissus, rockets and spaceships, airplanes, naval vessels, businesses, and the arms of war. Mythology became a key that helped to unlock the meaning of the language that surrounds them.

Our use of mythology as an integrating theme allowed us to respond to what Robert Coles (1988) terms "the call of stories." Stories—especially myths, which were the very first stories—contain truths we need to discover in our own lives and in the world around us. Each one of us has a story—an accumulation of relationships, feelings, experiences, events, dreams, and destinies—that make up who and what we are. Our stories are as unique as every other aspect of our beings, and yet each has a thread, the thread of human experience, that ties us to every other story that has ever been or will be.

The process of responding to the call of stories is, for me, the essence and purpose of using literature in my classroom. It is not about simply giving my students entertaining, well-written, "real" stories to read so that I can ask them questions about structure and content. We are *responding to the call*. I want my literature-based curriculum to do what myths have done for thousands of years—to give children the power to create meaning in their lives and to recognize our stories as one.

References

Burnett, Frances Hodgson. 1987. *The Secret Garden*. Boston: David Godine.

Campbell, Joseph. 1969. *The Masks of God*. New York: Penguin.

Coles, Robert. 1988. *The Call of Stories.* Boston: Houghton Mifflin.

Colum, Padraic. 1946. *The Children's Homer.* New York: Collier.

D'Aulaire, Ingri, and Edgar D'Aulaire. 1967. *D'Aulaire's Book of Greek Myths.* New York: Scholastic.

Fisher, Leonard Everett. 1988. *Theseus and the Minotaur.* New York: Holiday House.

Gibson, Michael. 1977. *Gods, Men, and Monsters from Greek Myths.* New York: Schocken.

Lister, Robin. 1987. *The Odyssey.* New York: Doubleday.

Osborne, Will, and Mary Pope. 1988a. *Jason and the Argonauts.* New York: Scholastic.

———. 1988b. *The Deadly Power of Medusa.* New York: Scholastic.

Stillman, Peter R. 1985. *Introduction to Myth.* 2nd ed. Portsmouth, NH: Boynton/Cook.

ONCE UPON A TIME
IN ROOM SEVEN

KATHLEEN A. MOORE
Thorncliffe Elementary School
East York Board of Education
Toronto, Ontario

*T*old by sleepy guards beside a castle keep to help stave off sleep, by crones near the dying embers of a peasant cottage to close young eyes, by travelers to distract from aching feet, by peddlers to sell more wares, fairy tales have now been relegated to the nursery, told by grandmothers to our mothers and then to us. Will we tell them to our students so they too can "touch magic" and "pass it on" (Yolen 1981, 91)? Or will we ignore this literary genre for its outmoded values and story lines? What treasures lie dusty on our library shelves? And what can fairy tales contribute to our students' literacy?

One evening in January, I made a mistake that changed the course of the school year. I inadvertently agreed to make a presentation about fantasy, a subject I knew nothing about, to my fellow university students. The next day, during my grade-two class sharing time, Ghazala commented, "In my language, we celebrate this holiday by fasting during the day and by eating only after sunset."

Whenever Ghazala talks to me about her family, church, or special days, she prefaces her remarks with the phrase "in my language." At first, I thought it sounded quaint and inexact, but I realized that when I hear Vassiliki and Fotini speaking Greek, I can imagine I am in the agora in Athena. When Reshma and Ghazala chat and giggle, I am in a market on the outskirts of Karachi. When Alexia and Rhea regale us with a story about Trinidad, we are there on the beach with them as they recall allnight cookouts. Language. Not just letters, not just words or sentences, but the heartbeat of our shared experiences. If Ghazala believed that "in my language" is all she needed to help me bridge the gap between our cultures, why couldn't "once upon a time long, long ago" create a bridge to help Ghazala and the rest of my students enter the world of fantasy?

While frantically trying to become an instant expert for my university course presentation, I began reading *The Lion, the Witch and the Wardrobe* to my class. It seemed a bold act at the time: no booklists recommend Lewis's Narnia books for seven-year-olds. As the story unfolded, the children's interest deepened. Ordinarily, the vocabulary, manner of expression, and situations would have been beyond them. But they somehow sensed the power of the tale to create new worlds of experience. Tears rolled down Reshma's cheeks when Aslan died. Ghazala reported that when her own cupboard door creaked, she had wondered if she would find a strange land inside. Fotini saw a wardrobe in a furniture store and thought that if her dad bought it, she too could enter Narnia. André spied a tent in a camping store display that reminded him of Lucy and Susan in Aslan's tent, and when Vassiliki wore her fuzzy sweater, she remembered Aslan's soft fur. The children began to play Narnia games at recess. For my students, Lewis's wardrobe provided a way into a new land. Their own experiences had not altered, but their perceptions of them had.

Meanwhile, my professional reading had begun to disclose fascinating information about fairy tales. Bettelheim (1976) commented that primers and preprimers may teach skills and some children's literature might inform or entertain, but fairy tales enrich the inner life of the child (4). Jane Yolen (1981) explained, "The best of the old stories spoke to the listener because they spoke not only to the ears but to the heart as well" (25). Such a belief led her to the conviction that in ignoring fairy tales we deny our students "access to their inheritance of story" (20). And Jack Zipes (1983) wrote that the fairy tale may be "the most important cultural and social event in most children's lives" (1).

I had ignored fairy tales in my own reading and in my teaching of reading. My parents had read to me the usual classics as bedtime stories, but magic was not a valued commodity in my no-nonsense family. I had wandered far from fairyland when I realized that folk literature can provide a "landscape of allusion" (Yolen, 17), a way of understanding other cultures and other times, a scaffolding for other beliefs and our own. I felt that I could not afford to ignore fairy tales any longer.

During my book sharing time, I began to read fairy tales aloud.

The rapport between my students and the tales was instant. I was surprised to learn that, except for a few encounters with Walt Disney versions, even the familiar tales were new to my students. Whatever had been read at home, it certainly had not been fairy tales. With a fresh enthusiasm, they rejoiced over Cinderella's good fortune, were both frightened and amused by the wolf in Little Red Riding Hood, felt in awe of the prince's brave quest for Sleeping Beauty, and hated the queen for her jealousy of Snow White. The children began to choose and read fairy tales for themselves during our reading workshop. The school librarian wanted to show how the themes in fairy tales are universal, so she began to read fairy tales from other lands during our weekly library visits. I continued to read my own favorite fairy tales to the class. We were each beginning to trace the lines and whorls of these "thumbprints of history" (Yolen, 30).

At the top of a piece of chart paper, I wrote "Fairy Tales." I posted the chart near the sharing corner so that as we read and talked, we could keep a record of what we found out about the genre. I was curious to learn what aspects of the fairy tales the children considered most crucial to the success of the stories. Eleni suggested that without a problem, "there would be no story." Most agreed with this opinion but offered other suggestions.

Fotini commented that a wicked person was essential because "if there's no bad person then there's nothing to fight against." Zaid added, "When you meet a bad person in a tale you know there's going to be danger, and it makes the story better." Ghazala thought that if there were no hero, "there wouldn't be anyone to do the rescuing." Reshma mentioned that love is important because "if there's no love there would be no marriage and no happy ending." She also reminded us that many stories begin with parents loving a daughter very much. Imraan thought that "things or people have to change or the story doesn't go anywhere," and many concurred that magic was necessary so that "ordinary things could become special." Nadir liked it when punishment was meted out because "the evil people deserve it." Everyone agreed that fairy tales need to begin with "once upon a time" or "in a far-off land long, long ago" to let us know we would be reading a fairy tale and not an ordinary story.

These discussions showed me that the children were beginning to notice and appreciate the special features of the tales. Fairy tales were becoming familiar enough for them to be able to stand back, view them as a body of work, compare and contrast elements of structure, and decide what made the tales effective stories for them as individual readers with idiosyncratic interests and preferences.

When I inquired, I was astounded by the number of versions of the same story many of the students had read. Ghazala had read two renditions of Beauty and the Beast but preferred the one in which the beast made promises to Beauty's father. Ladi discovered that one of the versions of Snow White included a description of her death. Fotini found a Cinderella story with a detailed account of Cinderella's early life when her mother was still alive. Reshma preferred the ugly duckling story in which the duckling's travels in search of acceptance were detailed. Altogether, my students had read more than one version of thirty-four different tales. Quietly, independently, they had been conducting their own studies of the evolutionary journeys of these ancient tales. "How is this version different?" became a frequent question during book sharing.

One day, Reshma brought to the sharing circle a fairy tale she had written herself. The other children soon began to try their hand at writing their own fairy tales, using the recurring themes they had recognized in their reading. This writing proved to be not so much a product of reading fairy tales as a brief stopping place for reflection before they continued reading.

In my class, I scheduled time for book talks so that in the course of a week every student had a chance to tell us about a book he or she had read that week. Their discussions roved over the fairy tale literature. As both participant and eavesdropper, I heard them despair with Rapunzel trapped in the tower, with Sleeping Beauty cursed by a long sleep, with Snow White evading the jealous queen, with Cinderella contending with spiteful step-sisters. They rejoiced when Rapunzel healed her prince's blind-ness with her tears, when the prince courageously forged his way to Sleeping Beauty's palace, when Gretel pushed the witch into the oven. They wondered why the little mermaid would endure pain to become what she was not, why the ugly duckling did not realize earlier that he was really beautiful, why the Snow Queen wanted Kay, why the witch turned the prince into a frog. The tales stirred their curiosity. They questioned me, each other, and even the tellers of the tales when they felt puzzled by an unpredictable turn of events. Suddenly these seven-year-olds were discussing literature at a level I had not dreamed possible.

As the students responded in their reading journals, they affirmed that almost all the fairy tales began with a problem. Goldilocks' problem was that she was too curious. The difficulties in Rapunzel began when the mother wished for the rampion belonging to the witch, and in Sleeping Beauty when the twelfth fairy felt insulted. The problem in The Nightingale was the emperor's preference for the artificial over the real. Once the problem had been identified, it was just a short step for the children to appreciate how the teller of the tale had resolved it. Discussing Rapunzel, Eleni and Fotini believed that it was the prince's love for Rapunzel's singing that gave him the courage to rescue her from the tower. Reshma and Ghazala decided that the prince must have been very brave to overcome such dangerous obstacles to reach Sleeping Beauty. The children found that although magic often occurred in tales, it was really the characters' great love or courage or persistence that won the day.

From my students' response journals I learned which fairy tales were favorites and why. Afzal admired the bravery of Jack climbing the beanstalk. Reshma was especially interested in the pain the little mermaid would endure "just for a man." She continued to read, wondering if the mermaid would still "care about the prince." Fotini noticed the similarity between Cinderella and Snow White: "First they made me sad and then they made me very happy. I also wished I could be a princess so that the witch couldn't hurt me." As Nadir discussed his entry about the ugly duckling with me, he described the part about the bird becoming beautiful, then spread out his own arms like wings to show how it must have felt. I was impressed by the specificity with which the children described their favorites and how unhesitatingly they zeroed in on what caught their attention in each.

Then I asked my students, "If you had to recommend five fairy tales not to be missed by other readers, which would you choose?" Every student had his or her own "best" list. I also asked them to pinpoint those parts of the story not to be skipped by other readers, so that I could discover more about the children's interaction with text. At first they seemed puzzled by this question. They said other readers would need to read the whole story. I explained, "It's like a special TV show where you tell your friend not to be visiting the refrigerator during certain parts of the story." They grinned with understanding and promptly began to pour out not-to-be-missed highlights. The students unerringly focused on what was, for them, the high spot in each story—when Sleeping Beauty woke up, when the prince found the owner of the glass slipper, when the duckling discovered he was the swan, when Sleeping Beauty met the dwarfs so "she wouldn't be lonely," when the frog turned back into a prince.

The details of the stories were sharp and clear, easily retrieved from memory and accessible for discussion. As ideas were expressed, the others agreed, thought of additional stories, and discussed why the parts mentioned were highlights. Their enthusiasm was refreshingly spontaneous. No one remained silent or uninvolved. They were all such authorities in this field that each could make a valuable contribution to the information being discussed.

Reshma speaks fluent Gujarati as well as English. Between January and March, she read thirty-two fairy tales. In February, she discovered a book of Pakistani stories in our library. Months later, Reshma retold the story of Ram for us in her writing. Some of the other students had already heard parts of it in Urdu and Hindi from grandparents and other older relatives. The stories are epic in nature, centuries old and contained in "a big old book like the Bible," Reshma explained. The students listened because they knew that fairy tales could be familiar paths that suddenly take strange and mystical turnings. Reshma read:

> Birith's eyes burned with rage when his mother banished his brother, Ram, to the forest. Birith announced that he would search for his beloved brother, Ram. Many people wanted to go along and so they did. When Birith finally found him, Ram was filled with joy.

Reshma is inheriting not only the gift of storying but the roots of her own culture.

At our annual Open House, when parents come to view their children's work and special displays, I had the opportunity to chat with them about their children's reading. Many reported a reversal of the usual circumstance at bedtime storytelling. Now my students were telling their parents, "Sit down. I have a new story to read to you." Through fairy tales, children and parents bridged not only the generation gap, but the gap between the centuries.

When I looked back on our fairy-tale odyssey, I saw how the early buds of curiosity blossomed and bore fruit. The stories of this new genre so resonated with the children's own budding experiences of life that I began to understand why they had been preserved for so long. They struck a chord of familiarity in the hearts of their readers; their similar form and characterization captured the imagination of my young readers, proving that "these stories are part of a lively fossil that refuses to die" (Yolen, 27).

I have changed my mind about the place of fairy tales in my

teaching. They will become an essential component of my students' literary heritage. The common body of work provides a basis for a shared forum of discussion, as students can discuss differences and similarities in characterization and plot by referring to stories we all know. The tightly knit structure of each narrative encourages beginning readers to press on to complete the whole story, and the patterns in the stories enhance predictability. If one part is obscure, students find they can pick up the story line on the next pages and bring fresh understanding to the more difficult passages. Familiar elements invite young readers rather than exclude them. Children who had been reading only picture books, relying heavily on illustrative cues to comprehend text, are delighted to discover they can read a whole story depending on text alone to provide the meaning.

Fairy tales, which deal with so many of the main themes of life—yearning, disappointment, courage, jealousy, birth, love, marriage, death, alienation, triumph, evil, goodness, cruelty—allowed my students to begin to come to grips with the human condition. The tales deepened their interactions with literature and also provided another window on a life previously glimpsed in adult conversations, TV sitcoms, or soaps. The stories were easy to remember and easy to retell. Stories beginning "once upon a time" or "in a far-off land" immediately placed the characters, plots, and themes at a sufficiently remote distance to allow full involvement without personal threat. Something of a paradox!

Once upon a time, not long ago, my students took a far journey to somewhere else, somewhere important. Like so many of the characters they met along the way, they were touched by magic. They became the princes and princesses of their own literary kingdoms.

References

Bettelheim, Bruno. 1976. *The Uses of Enchantment.* New York: Alfred A. Knopf.

Lewis, C. S. 1965. *The Lion, the Witch and the Wardrobe.* London: Collins.

Yolen, Jane. 1981. *Touch Magic.* New York: Philomel.

Zipes, Jack. 1983. *Fairy Tales and the Art of Subversion.* London: Heinemann.

The Author Interview

JACK PRELUTSKY

AN INTERVIEW BY KATHY HERSHEY

*I*t was a beautiful spring morning when I drove to Cincinnati to interview Jack Prelutsky. I was nervous but kept reminding myself that I was prepared. I'd read and reread most of his forty books of poetry, drafted and revised my interview questions, and packed my trusty tape recorder and two sets of batteries. None of these precautions could offset the fact that I'd never interviewed anyone other than my fourth-grade students, and here I was about to talk with Jack Prelutsky, a writer loved by children everywhere for his witty, imaginative poetry.

I had no idea what to expect when I met Jack in the lobby of his hotel, but my first reaction was to be charmed. As we chatted over brunch, it became evident that Jack's mercurial mind was not always going to move in sync with my carefully orchestrated questions. He noticed everything and was alert to anything out of the ordinary. A waitress walked by wearing a pin that read "Champion Server," which led to a discussion of brass trumpets, Sir Lancelot, and Ivan Lendl. These topics were not on my list, but they gave me insight into Jack's facility for noting details and making associations.

I had also failed to anticipate Jack's tongue-in-cheek sense of humor. I giggled through a good part of the interview and found myself quickly reduced to a childlike state. I think it's this very quality that makes Jack's poetry so enticing to kids. He's one of them.

When I finished the interview I was exhausted. It wasn't until later that I realized I'd captured on tape what I wanted—the essence of a poet at work. Jack is the embodiment of his poetry. He lives and breathes it.

As I transcribed our talk, it also became clear to me that teachers of language arts have to safeguard against getting too caught up in any one program or system. We need to offer kids lots of options and lots of time to find their own special talents and interests. Young writers and readers should feel safe enough to take risks and try new things. When we invite individuality and idiosyncrasy, we may find the Jack Prelutskys in our classrooms.

KATHY: How would you describe your childhood?

JACK: I was born in Brooklyn, but I actually grew up in the Bronx. I was small and unattractive as a child. I had buck teeth and big ears. I was little and skinny. I was unusually smart, even for a Jewish kid.

KATHY: Did you like school?

JACK: Well, I was a very shy and private person. I had an unfortunate combination of being very small, very smart, and having a big mouth. And living in a tough, blue-collar neighborhood, I got into a lot of fights, which I mostly lost. School was dreary. It was in an unattractive neighborhood. It was noisy.

KATHY: Were you a reader back then?

JACK: Yes, I was always a reader. I was a very introspective kid. I read a wide range of things when I was young. When I was about ten I got into the knights of armor stage. I loved *King Arthur*. I probably read it a dozen times.

KATHY: What were other influences during your elementary school years, besides reading?

JACK: My first love was music. I always loved music and, oddly, not the sort of music you would think. Not rock music, not popular music, not jazz, but opera. I used to sing along with Enrico [Caruso] when I was a kid. My father had a collection of Caruso records. So by the time I was twelve years old I knew a dozen tenor arias by heart. I had no idea what I was singing or what they were from or what it meant, but I could sing them. I was going to be an opera singer. I once had a beautiful voice, and I could have been an opera singer, but I wasn't going to be a Pavarotti. I had to decide what to do, so I went with the poetry because I could do something unique and special, whereas I would always have been a second best, or third best, singer.

KATHY: Did you have any other interests back then?

JACK: Yes, another thing I loved was arithmetic. It's funny, because now I tend to be a right-brain person, where the creative side dominates. But there was a time that I think I was also very left-brain. I was always at the top of the class in math. I never did homework. I remember being sent to the office because I finished a very difficult problem before the teacher finished it at the board. I had figured out some alternate way of doing it.

KATHY: Did you enjoy poetry in school?

JACK: Well, there wasn't much stuff around that kids could relate to. Most of the poetry we had to study had nothing to do with growing up in the 1940s in New York City.

KATHY: Was poetry more enjoyable later on, in high school?

JACK: I sort of liked the sonnets. I remember liking "Much have I traveled in the realms of gold and many goodly states and kingdoms. . . ." I kind of got into that. But I found most of the teaching methods tedious. I remember having to read "Idylls of the King" and all the Tennyson stuff. I couldn't get into it. I still don't know what an antispast is. I only know what iambic pentameter is because somebody once pointed out to me that I'd never written a poem in that form. So I wrote one in *Headless Horseman*. As a kid I didn't like poetry but I loved words, language, word puzzles, crosswords. Anything we could make up.

KATHY: The range of your poetry is incredible. How do you come up with ideas for poems?

JACK: I do a lot of free associating. I was sitting next to a woman on the plane yesterday, and I noticed she was putting on lipstick. She just kept putting it on and putting it on. So I sat there and thought lipstick, lipstick. This is going to be part of a poem I'm writing for adults. I also just look at someone and start writing things down—crow's feet, wrinkled lips, long fingernails. Then I'll decide what the dominant features are.

Another example is a poem from my new book, *Something Big Has Been Here*. It's the sequel to *New Kid on the Block*. There's a poem in there about a creature called "The Addle-pated Paddlepuss." It's a creature that plays ping-pong with its face. It's based on a variety of experiences. I started thinking about ping-pong because I was playing it with a fellow in a basement in Eugene, Oregon. He was a spectacular player. He'd spot me nineteen points and beat me twenty-one to nineteen. He'd play with a smaller paddle or half the table and still beat me. That led me to remember Ping-Pong Parlor in New York City where world-class players played, and they'd play with their wallets and still beat me. (I'm just an average, basement player.) Then I remembered going to the zoo when I was a kid and seeing the platypus. I started thinking—the plate puss. Then I recalled watching a television show as a kid called "You Asked for It," and they brought on a cat who played ping-pong. So I combined all of these ideas. A cat who played ping-pong led to a cat-a-puss and then platapuss, paddlepuss. This led me to remember all those ping-pong players who lived to play ping-pong. I wrote:

> The Addle-pated Paddlepuss
> is agile as a cat,
> its neck is long and limber,
> and its face is broad and flat,
> it moves with skill and vigor,
> with velocity and grace,
> as it spends its every second
> playing ping-pong with its face.

I end the poem by saying:

> If you're fond of playing ping-pong
> and would like to lose in style,
> the Addle-pated Paddlepuss
> will serve you for awhile.

KATHY: It's fascinating to see how you gather all these ideas and then combine them with rhythm and rhyme.

JACK: I work very hard perfecting it as a craft. I think words themselves are fun. I'm very conscious of the sounds of things. For poets and writers in general, sounds are at least as important as meanings. I do use a rhyming dictionary. It's a tool for me, like a carpenter uses a tape measure. It's my second most-used reference book.

KATHY: What are your feelings about students wanting to make their poetry rhyme?

JACK: Don't let them do it. They have few skills to start with, and poetry is hard. They also have few experiences to draw on. They want to write the rhyme and the rest of the poem and no meaning. It just gets in the way of what they want to say.

Writing comes a lot easier for me now. I've written more poems in the last five years than I wrote in the previous twenty.

Now I'm more aware of what I'm doing and more aware of children. When I started working, I wrote for myself. Now I listen to children and have them in mind when I write. I try to give voice to some of the things they have inside. I don't moralize. Sometimes I'm criticized for writing about things like food fights. But what I do is observe kids and in my poems say, "This is what you're doing. You're being a child." I think children need a voice like that.

KATHY: Did you have any formal training in writing or did you pick it up on your own?

JACK: Even though I was a very quick study, I had no discipline. Didn't study and rarely did homework. I had working-class parents who didn't finish high school themselves and were unaware of the importance of homework. Writing was a chore, and I didn't like poetry. I had a junior high teacher who overanalyzed poetry—really overanalyzed and killed works of art that way. I liken it to dissecting frogs in biology.

In high school I had one very good English teacher who briefly awakened my interest in poetry. Because I was also a singer, I went to the High School of Music and Art in New York. I started listening to the words of the songs. I also memorized the words to two hundred stupid rock songs because they were "the thing." It was a natural part of my life; it was fun. Now if teachers could only do the same thing with poetry and make it part of their students' lives.

KATHY: It seems like your training was mostly outside the system.

JACK: It really was. I went on to flunk English I twice in college. Some of my strongest influences were folk music. I was a coffee house folk singer in the early sixties. I sang English, Irish, Scottish, and Appalachian ballads. Unlike rock music, the words stood on their own without the music. They were written by ordinary people.

I really have worked outside the system. I was probably more influenced by Groucho Marx than by Shakespeare. I gave a speech a couple of months ago at the New York Public Library on the creative process. I was on a series with Katherine Paterson, Jean Fritz, Rosemary Wells, Maurice Sendak, and Jill Krementz. Each of us had to produce a bibliography of about thirty works that influenced our writing. Everyone else was so serious. I wrote my entire bibliography in rhyme. I listed Bill Cosby, Woody Allen, Groucho, Lewis Carroll, and S. J. Perelman. (I had to drive them a little crazy.) But when I looked at my list, there were hardly any poets on it. Of all the persons who had influenced my work, very few ever wrote two lines that rhymed.

And I never did finish college. So, yes, I did work outside of the system.

KATHY: Since you seem to operate intuitively, do you write that way or do you adhere to a schedule?

JACK: What do you think?

KATHY: That you write when you want to write.

JACK: Sometimes I go for months without writing, and I feel no need to write.

KATHY: Does this worry you?

JACK: No, I used to worry that I'd dry up, but I compare it to the way a farmer plants a field. There are people who have to write every day or they get sick. Some are driven. Some are like me and have no discipline. Everyone's different. So a farmer plants his field in the spring, and for me the planting is the ideas. In the summer the things grow. Then in the fall you harvest, and in the winter you let things lie fallow for a while and then you start over.

The spring is taking notes, and I have a year-round spring. I use these small notebooks about the size of my hand for notes. I keep all of them in a fireproof file. If I stack them up they're taller than I am. So far I've only used maybe ten percent of all the stuff in my notebooks. Spring is also thinking about things. Summer is when notes are taken and enlarged upon. Harvest is the actual writing of poems. Then I'm drained, just like a field is drained, and I sort of let it sit.

I have no schedule. When I don't work I just go about my business. I do take notes year round, and it's a rare day I don't have something down—maybe a word or a joke. Some are bare outlines of poems. Some may just be a couplet or series of ideas.

KATHY: Did you write *Something Big Has Been Here* because you felt you'd collected enough ideas, and it was time for another book?

JACK: When I work, I work feverishly around the clock, sixteen hours a day or more. I can't sleep. I live in my bathrobe. I just work and work and work. I wrote *The New Kid on the Block* in seven weeks working around the clock. Some of the notes were from ten years earlier. When I finished I had more than I started with because each poem gives birth to two more poems as new ideas come out of it.

The sequel to *New Kid on the Block* took a year, but actual sitting-down time was about two months. I had reached a point when I thought I had enough ideas for the sequel, but when I got it together I realized I only had enough for about thirty poems. Then the work really started, and I drew from the last five or ten years. I reached a sticking point at about forty or fifty poems, and I couldn't write another poem. I went blank for a couple of months. I couldn't write anything. Then suddenly it all came back, and I wrote the last fifty poems in about two weeks. I just went insane.

KATHY: I'm really curious about your working relationships with your illustrators.

JACK: Well, they're all different. I've been very lucky with illustrators who've had their own clear vision. The last few years I worked with Arnold Lobel. *Tyrannosaurus Was a Beast* was the last book he illustrated before he died. We used to meet for lunch in New York and talk about the book. Or we might call each other. Then he'd just go do it. We did seven books together. I had six small suggestions to make to him out of the entire seven books. In one instance I asked him to make a creature scarier. He was so good.

Another of my illustrators is James Stevenson, whom I've neither met nor spoken to. We did *The Baby Uggs Are Hatching* and *The New Kid on the Block*. I made a special trip to New York just to see the illustrations for *New Kid*, and there were two dozen I didn't like. Some were misinterpreted or too adult. Two days later he had two dozen new illustrations, and I still hadn't spoken to him. He's doing *Something Big Has Been Here*.

On the other end is Garth Williams. We became good friends. He's a very interesting man.

I lived in Albuquerque, and he was living in Santa Fe at the time. A mutual friend introduced us and we hit it off. My wife says he's like an old me. I was in on almost his entire creative process. I'd go up once or twice a week for lunch or dinner and see the progress of the drawings—make criticisms and talk about them. That's as close as I've ever been to actually illustrating a book myself. He's also doing the illustrations for *Underneath a Blue Umbrella*.

KATHY: When you have time to read, what kinds of books do you choose?

JACK: I read a lot of contemporary fiction. I read a lot of the younger writers to see what's going on. I also have certain favorites. For example, I've read almost everything that Isaac Bashevis Singer has ever written. I eagerly await each of his new books. I read S. J. Perelman, natural history such as animal studies, science fiction, lots of humor. I read all the children's poetry books, and I buy them all. I read a lot of odd books of odd facts, and trivia collections. They're idea mills for me. I buy art books and subscribe to the *New Yorker* and *Atlantic Monthly*. I read a lot on crafts. I subscribe to *Fine Woodworking Magazine*. I love it. I also subscribe to game magazines. I read about three books a week.

KATHY: Many of your poems relate to food, so I guess you like to cook.

JACK: Yes, I love to cook and read cookbooks. I like to cook and eat ethnic cuisines—Chinese, Japanese, East Indian, Italian, and French. I like a good matzo ball soup. I tend to cook ethnic food or make something up. It's not always universally successful.

KATHY: Is cooking relaxing for you?

JACK: Yes, it is. It's therapy. I like to cook for friends, but I'm kind. I only serve maybe one experimental dish.

KATHY: What do you see yourself doing in future years?

JACK: I don't think I'll ever retire. There are things I want to do as I cut back on traveling. But I'll continue to write books of humorous verse for adults—try to be an Ogden Nash a little bit. I also want to write prose for children. I'd also like to write a musical comedy for children and maybe later for adults. Maybe it won't happen, but I have a good idea for one. I want to do some more recording and produce the tape myself. I want to be a woodworker and actually make and design furniture and sell it. I also want to spend more time with my photography again. I want to have fun making odd objects—machines that do nothing. I have hundreds of thousands of little artifacts around the house for collages. And I want to travel a lot and write some travel books. Maybe they'll be funny ones, or maybe they'll be for children. I don't know.

Mostly, I want to create. I want to make photographs and make furniture and make art. Just do those things I've always been driven to do. I also want to go back and take some voice lessons and sing with a nice chorus. I'd like to live in the country somewhere. Just create and not be bothered.

KATHY: It's interesting that even though you don't force your life into any structured pattern, you are very goal-oriented.

But they're goals you set for yourself. And you don't force a time line or deadline.

JACK: No, I don't. My goals change. Some of the things I said I wanted to do I may not have wanted to do a few years ago. There are probably a couple of things around the corner I'm not aware of yet. That's one thing I try to impress on kids, too: that they have things inside they don't know anything about yet.

KATHY: What kind of advice would you give teachers to help students find their own special strengths?

JACK: I believe in serendipity. You never know what skills are going to be valuable. My only advice is to keep your eyes and ears open. And take notes! If you see somebody walk down the street with a penguin on his head, write it down. One of the main differences between a writer and a nonwriter is a writer knows he's not going to remember the next day what happened.

The other thing is, don't be afraid to try new things. The thing you may love to do may not even exist yet. I always leave myself open to possibilities. Who knows, maybe one day I'll want to sky dive. There may be some art form that has something to do with computers that I'm unaware of; it may exist tomorrow. Maybe I'll try to compose music using computers.

That's one of the things about books that are so important. There's so much knowledge out there, more than any one person could accumulate in a lifetime. Books can give you a taste of it that nothing else can.

Learning is the most important thing to me. When kids ask me which of my books is my favorite, I tell them it's the book that I'm working on. They say, what book is that? I say it doesn't matter, and they don't understand. Then I have to explain process versus product. Once I've written a book, it's finished, my name is on it, and I feel good about it, but there's nothing more I can do about it. It's the end product. For me the process is important because that's when I'm learning and figuring things out. It's a great joy to do it, to write.

The day I stop enjoying the process is the day I stop writing.

So whatever book I'm working on is my favorite book because that's the one that's alive. Before a book is between covers it's alive inside a person. That person is exploring and finding new ways of saying things and seeing new things.

It's the same thing with your life in general and opening up. It's being aware of all the things that are out there.

Books Mentioned in the Interview

The Headless Horseman Rides Tonight: More Poems to Trouble Your Sleep. New York: Greenwillow, 1980. Illustrated by Arnold Lobel.

The Baby Uggs Are Hatching. New York: Greenwillow, 1982. Illustrated by James Stevenson.

The New Kid on the Block. New York: Greenwillow, 1984. Illustrated by James Stevenson.

Tyrannosaurus Was a Beast. New York: Greenwillow, 1988. Illustrated by Arnold Lobel.

Underneath a Blue Umbrella. New York: Greenwillow. To be released in spring of 1990.

Something Big Has Been Here. New York: Greenwillow. To be released in fall of 1990.

AUDIENCE: KEY TO WRITING ABOUT READING

CYRENE WELLS
High Street School
Pembroke, New Hampshire

*T*he first year I tried a reading workshop format with my seventh- and eighth-grade students, I read, reread, and dog-eared the pages of Nancie Atwell's *In the Middle* (1987). I put together a plan based on the book with a few modifications. Students would choose what they read, and they would be required to write me a letter at least once a week in dialogue journals. "Tell me what you're thinking as you read your books," I instructed them. "Explain when you don't understand something. I'm here to help."

I am not sure that I admitted it to myself at the time, but my major goal for the dialogue journals was to make sure that the kids were reading. I wanted to be certain they understood what they read, and I wanted proof (on paper) that they were actually doing something in that quiet classroom. Assessment is a necessary component of a reading program, but I realize now that I allowed it to overshadow the intrinsic value of the letters. When I did consider dialogue journals as a vehicle for learning, I thought more in terms of what I could teach students through my responses to their letters than what they might learn through the process of writing them.

For the most part, students complied with the requirement to write to me about their reading. Once things were going well, I decided to take what I thought was the next step: I asked them to write to one another. I had purposely waited to encourage peer correspondence because I wanted to make sure my students were on the right track, that they knew how to write "good" letters before they started writing to each other. In November,

I put examples of peer letters from Atwell's book on the over-head projector. Students were interested; it was a bit like reading someone else's mail. Doing it themselves, however, was another matter. They saw writing to each other as superfluous. In the two months before I introduced the idea of peer writing, they had discovered what this letter writing stuff was all about: my assessment of their work. I had established myself as *the* correspondent. Writing to friends did not fit in this context.

I probably should have anticipated what happened next. Some students did write to other students, mostly for social purposes; others wrote identical letters to me and to their friends. Some wanted to know what they would "get" for writing. (I had already told them that their grades would be based on the frequency and quality of the letters written to me.) A few students, still in shock over having to write letters at all, could not believe that I would ask them to write more. "You mean, we got to write you, and then we got to write somebody else too? About the same book?"

I don't remember that I pushed very hard after the initial resistance. I suspect that I was as happy as the students were with the status quo. It was very orderly. And, while I don't think I was consciously aware of the narrowness of my goals for letter writing, I was still working hard to meet them.

The year progressed and, despite the lack of peer dialogues, there were successes. Students did write personal responses to specific characters and plots in their letters to me. They questioned authors' techniques and choices. They discussed dialogue, structure, and genre. They also operated an oral, informal system of referring books to one another. They whispered over titles, huddled in corners, and did a lot of miming and pointing during the time for quiet reading: "I'm not talking. I'm just telling her about a book."

Yet, even as other aspects of my classes were going well, I increasingly regretted that we had given up using the journals for peer dialogue. The limitations were obvious. For one thing, I didn't know all the answers; I didn't even know all the questions. For another, I suspected that students weren't stretching themselves or, for that matter, having much fun with the letters. More than a few developed patterns for their letters, filling in names and places as their current books dictated. In turn, I found myself responding in a predictable manner. We not only lacked spontaneity, but we often cheated ourselves of genuine involvement as readers and responders.

The key was audience. I had learned from researchers such as Graves (1989), Calkins (1983), Atwell (1987), and Romano (1987), and through my own experiences with student writers, that audience is crucial to the act of writing. When writers have a variety of audiences, they must accommodate different opinions or understandings of what is being said. With a specific audience in mind, the writer finds his or her voice; real communication takes place because the writer predicts the reader's response as he or she composes. Because of the way I set up the journal-writing aspect of the reading workshop, I had limited the audience to myself—not a horrible audience for some purposes but certainly a limited one. My students, who doggedly wrote only for me, taught me that I was not enough, that audience is as important to the writing of dialogue journals as it is to fiction, poetry, and other nonfiction. This was something I had not considered when I started. We needed to broaden the audience for writing about reading.

The next autumn there was no warm-up period for peer writing. I explained it the first day of school. Students would be required to write to one another at least once a week; they would also have to write to me once a week.

Initially, the letters between friends were stilted. Students were not used to passing notes about books (especially in spiral-bound notebooks). Jim wrote to me after he'd written his first letter to his friend Marc: "I don't know about this writing to our friends. It's hard to write to a friend because you don't want to sound stupid about what you write." Then, too, they were writing to one another knowing that I would also see the letters. It was hard to be natural.

I worked to make the unnatural seem natural. For one thing, students needed to see how everyone else was handling it. During those early weeks I often asked letter writers' permission to put correspondence on the overhead projector. I used letters to me and my responses as well as letters between students. I showed letters about book recommendations, letters between students who were reading the same books, and letters that complained about plot or characters. I wanted the students to see various approaches and subjects for literary correspondence. There were no perfect letters, no wrong letters, just letters that showed thinking.

Although it was sometimes difficult for me, I made a point, especially in the beginning, not to interfere with what students wrote to one another—even when the letters were pure silliness.

We needed to develop a trust, not just between students and teacher but among students too. Perhaps because of the models I'd shown them, or because students had no choice about the peer writing component, or because it was essentially more fun than just writing to me, peer letters began to work, and soon it was routine to write and respond to a number of people each week. With peer dialogue in place, my education began.

I found that most students wrote differently to their friends than they did to me: "I'm still reading *The Diary of a Young Girl.* It's long and boring, and I'm going to get it finished by tomorrow. Mrs. Wells and my mother are on my back." Often the subject would be the same in letters to me and friends, but the slant would be different. For instance, Joanne wrote me an intense letter explaining her reaction to *Charlotte's Web.* Later the same day, when she wrote to Marcia, she approached it from a more personal angle.

Dear Mrs. Wells,

I'm reading *Charlotte's Web* by E. B. White. I love it so much. It touched me when the spider dies and when the other animals tease him. I know how it is to be teased. It is like in the movies when some one gets whipped. What are you gonna do? You know it hurts them, but what do you do? When Wilber got out earlier in the book when he was running around, my heart was racing so fast because I didn't want him to get hurt even though he didn't.

Joanne

Dear Marcia,

I'm reading *Charlotte's Web.* I would have hated to be Fern and have to sell Wilber (the pig). Because we found a dog, kept it for about 3 weeks, and then we got rid of it. I was very sad. You know what I mean? 'Cause what if you had to give up Barney or Ginger? You would be sad, right? Am I right?

Jo

Readers would also seek out friends who had read or were reading the book they were writing about: "What was your favorite part? Mine was when Rob left. I was almost crying." "What did you think of the ending? My sister said it was stupid, but I haven't got that far yet."

What a reader thought of a book, author, or topic often directed whom he or she chose to write to: "I am reading the book called *If This Is Love, I'll Take Spaghetti* by Ellen Conford. It has nine different stories in it. It's mainly romance stories. I would think cause you like romance this book is for you." Graves (1989) says that in letter writing, students deal with "Who are you, who am I, who are we together?" and that the writer signals the reader that both are present in the text. Choice of writing partners then sets the stage for dialogue unique to that pair.

Some students wrote to a small circle of friends. Others, perhaps more social by nature, wrote to everyone. Although no one had an exclusive writing partner for the year, there were periods of time for almost all of them when they preferred writing to one friend more than others. Social happenings outside the class often determined who wrote to whom. "What's up? Boy you look good today. If Jeff doesn't ask you out, maybe I will. I'm reading *Rascal. . . .*" In the whole scheme of things, my role became less central. A student would write differently to me, perhaps in the same way he would write differently to Ronda than to Jeff. The writer would also expect a different kind of response from each of us.

Audience seemed to help the writer in two ways. The most obvious was through direct response—answering or asking questions and making comments. Zac and Dom, seventh-grade buddies who teamed up several times in writing workshop to tell stories about skateboarding and dirt bike racing, found that they enjoyed writing to one another:

Dear Dom,

What's up? Not that much here. Just reading an awesome, I mean awesome book. It is called *Where the Red Fern Grows*. I don't know where they got the title but it is not the best title for the book.

Zac

Dear Zac,

I'm reading *Double-Dare O'Toole* by Constance C. Greene. It's an ok book so far. It's about a boy who does everything he is dared to.

Your friend,
Dom

P.S. What would you give the book for a title?

Dear Dom,

The title I would give my book is *The Boy in the Ozarks*. Because that is where he's lived all his life and hunted and the mountains sound much better.

Dear Zac,

My title fits my book good, and do you think I should read that book when you're done?

Your friend,
Dom

Dom picked up on his friend's confusion about the title in an otherwise "awesome" book. In order to respond to Dom, Zac reviewed the book in a broad sense, titled it, and justified his decision. Later, when he reached the end of *Where the Red Fern Grows* and discovered Rawls' reason for the title, Zac had already considered title and had a context in which to judge it. Dom, too, gained from the exchange. He considered the appropriateness of his book's title and learned about another book he might enjoy.

Recommending books was one of the most common ways that friends directed one another's thinking. Often the student responding did more thinking than the writer of the original letter. In the following exchange Zac writes to Sadie, perhaps because she read more books than anyone else in their class.

Dear Sadie,

What's up? Not too much here. I'm reading *The Incredible Journey*. It's a good book. I'm almost finished and I'd like to know if you have any idea what I can read next. Tell me in your letter.

Zac

Okay Zac,

Well what kind of books do you like—fiction, nonfiction, science fiction? I like fiction the best—some books by Judy Blume, Lois Duncan, and *Bones on Black Spruce Mountain* by David Budbill. Only 126 pages and a good book. It's about this boy and his friend who go camping on Black Spruce Mountain and find some bones and tell all the stuff they did. I liked it even though it's more for boys.

Sadie

You can almost see Sadie's brain working. What kind of book would he like? I like. . . . and she ticks off authors she has enjoyed. Books, umm . . . *Black Spruce Mountain*! He'd probably like that. It's an outdoorsy book like *The Incredible Journey*, and I know he liked *Red Fern*. Then she baits the hook by describing the book. In the process, she has categorized books by author and subject matter and summarized a novel that is "more for boys" than girls.

Direct response, then, is one important way that audience contributes to a reader's understanding. Audience also plays another role, perhaps less tangible but equally important. The recipient of a letter, simply by being there, holds a place in the writer's mind. The writer must explain what he or she is reading in terms of the recipient's interests or prior knowledge. For example, when Marc writes to Eric, he explains himself in a postscript because while he knows what he's talking about, he has to make sure that Eric does, too.

> Dear Eric,
>
> I am reading *The Adventures of Ulysses* by Bernard Evslin. I can't really tell you much about it because I'm only on page 10. But Ulysses is a Viking adventurer and they're in a small town right now.
>
> Marc
>
> P.S. If you are wondering about who they are, it's him and his men who sail with him.

Zemelman and Daniels (1988) indicate that writing for a variety of audiences gives students "vital practice in thinking about their readers, trying to guess what they know, believe, understand, respond to, what language they recognize, what tone may be most effective with them" (23). The act of explaining, especially with a specific recipient in mind, seemed to help my students clarify their thinking. At the end of the year I asked students to explain what they saw as the connections between writing letters and understanding what they read. Michelle wrote:

> I think the connection between reading and writing in my journal is that it helps me understand my book. When I write a letter to a friend telling them about the book I think I'm actually telling myself about the book and explaining it to myself.

The process of explaining to oneself can be messy, repetitive, or disorganized. Based on a quick read-through, I thought that Christie was being redundant, scattered in her thinking when she wrote the following letter:

> Melissa,
>
> I'm reading *Nothing's Fair in the Fifth Grade* by Barthe DeClements. I'm on page 99. The chapter I'm on is called the Hitchhikers! This book is an OK book. It's a pretty good book. It's just that when I started reading the book it had a good lead and all but after the first few chapters the book started to drop. Then it rised again and now it's good! Maybe I'm starting to learn that the author does that just

to do that, and the author does that to get you interested in the book. Like the old saying goes—you learn a new thing everyday! Well gotta run! Bye.

Your friend always,
Christie

On closer examination, I decided that my first impression was exactly right *and* exactly the point. She is thinking as she writes, gathering and considering her ideas and clarifying her understanding, at the same time that she is writing for Melissa. Marcia, another student, explained it this way: "You have to learn to think and write at the same time."

Most students seemed to be aware that they were writing to think when they examined the connections between their dialogue journals and understanding what they had read:

"Sometimes I don't know it until I write it."

"It gives me time to think."

"It just makes you think twice."

The act of using writing to learn is often the subject of adult researchers. In our classroom students became researchers, actively noting how writing helps them think about what they read.

Students discovered another way that their diverse audiences helped them to think. Because the requirement of writing loomed over their heads, they read looking for things to write to various friends, classmates, and me. They were reading in order to write. Marc commented, "I learned to read more carefully so I could explain about it in my journal." His letters were short, very much to the point, and reflective: "I'm still reading *Bully of Barkham Street* by Mary Stolz. It's ok, nothing great. I think when the author wrote it, she paced it too slow and when I read it I start drifting off." For others, such as Christie in her letter to Melissa, writing was a chance to step away from a book long enough to reflect on it.

Christie, Mark, and my other students taught me a lot about dialogue journals in general and peer letters in particular. The first year, I discovered that writing to me was valuable, but the second year my students proved the larger value of choosing among an expanded audience of peers. At the very least, the increased volume of letter writing makes it more likely that students will reconsider what they have read, understanding their books and themselves better. More importantly, peer correspondence loosens up the process and lets readers and writers find voices that fit their audiences and audiences that fit their needs. I am glad I stepped away from being *the* correspondent.

There is a danger, I think, in following others' practices without really understanding them. I read Atwell's book, planned my program, but was initially unable to pull together the underlying theories. My goals for dialogue journals at the beginning of that first year, ones that revolved around assessment, were not wrong, but they were incomplete.

I needed to transfer my understanding of audience from such genres as poetry and fiction to the genre of letters. I needed to understand that some students will work much harder to explain their thinking to their friends (and thus themselves) than they will to me. I needed to see how students benefit from answering letters as well as generating them. And I needed to trust that students have things to teach to and learn from one another. When I clarified why I was doing what I was doing, established a structure for the exchanges, expected peer dialogues, and demonstrated how students could write to each other, I could back off from my central position as *the* audience and learn from my students.

References

Atwell, Nancie. 1987. *In the Middle: Writing, Reading, and Learning with Adolescents.* Portsmouth, NH: Boynton/Cook.

Budbill, David. 1984. *Bones on Black Spruce Mountain.* New York: Bantam.

Burnford, Sheila. 1961. *The Incredible Journey.* Boston: Little, Brown.

Calkins, Lucy M. 1983. *Lessons from a Child: On the Teaching and Learning of Writing.* Portsmouth, NH: Heinemann.

Conford, Ellen. 1983. *If This Is Love, I'll Take Spaghetti.* New York: Scholastic.

DeClements, Barthe. 1981. *Nothing's Fair in Fifth Grade.* New York: Viking.

Evslin, Bernard. 1969. *The Adventures of Ulysses.* New York: Scholastic.

Frank, Anne. 1953. *The Diary of a Young Girl.* New York: Doubleday.

Graves, Donald H. 1989. *Investigate Nonfiction,* The Reading/Writing Teacher's Companion series. Portsmouth, NH: Heinemann.

Greene, Constance C. 1981. *Double-Dare O'Toole.* New York: Dell.

North, Sterling. 1963. *Rascal.* New York: Dutton.

Rawls, Wilson. 1961. *Where the Red Fern Grows.* New York: Doubleday.

Romano, Tom. 1987. *Clearing the Way: Working with Teenage Writers.* Portsmouth, NH: Heinemann.

Stolz, Mary. 1963. *The Bully of Barkham Street.* New York: Dell.

White, E. B. 1952. *Charlotte's Web*. New York: Harper & Row.

Zemelman, Steven, and Harvey Daniels. 1988. *A Community of Writers: Teaching Writing in the Junior and Senior High School*. Portsmouth, NH: Heinemann.

TALK:
RESPONDING TO BOOKS
THE COLLABORATIVE WAY

ADELE FIDERER
Edgewood School
Scarsdale, New York

*M*ICHAEL: When Johnny saw Pumpkin Bean shot in the Common, what feelings do you think he felt?

DANNY: Mad.

MICHAEL: Why?

DANNY: Just because of the reason he was shot. It wasn't right. It just wasn't right!

MICHAEL: Yeah. I thought it was sort of a feeling of helplessness and fear—

DANNY: Yeah!

MICHAEL: —because he couldn't do anything—

DANNY: —because if he did, *he'd* be shot, and he just didn't want that to happen. He really felt badly about it.

This is "insider" talk that only readers of the book *Johnny Tremain* would understand. In this discussion, two fifth graders are trying to comprehend how Johnny felt when Pumpkin Bean, an English deserter he had befriended, was shot by the English during the Revolutionary War. Through talk, the insights expressed by one reader helped expand the thinking of the other. Talk also enabled each of the readers to explore his own thinking in an attempt to discover meaning. It is likely that neither Danny nor Michael was aware of how much he knew about the book until he heard himself. The flexibility of spoken language enabled the boys to reveal their full capacity for thinking and responding (Tough 1985).

It sounds so simple, so obvious. Yet for many years I was unaware that it was important to encourage students to talk

75

together in order to make sense of a book. My own experience as a member of an informal group of readers led me to see the value of a similar experience for my fourth- and fifth-grade students.

My friends and I get together for dinner every so often to talk about a book we've all read. After we've given our order to the waiter, we begin our discussion. At that point few of us agree about the worth of a book, or on its meaning. But as we listen to each other's interpretations, sometimes expressed with passion, we begin to consider other viewpoints and to think about the book in different ways. By the time coffee is served, each of us has an altered, deeper understanding of the book. For me and my friends, talking about a book with others seems necessary to complete the reading experience.

My book discussion group became a tentative model for the response experience I wanted my students to have. My students, like those described by Atwell (1984), choose their own books, read them in class, and write to me about their reading. I began to look for a way to extend my reading workshop to include purposeful, collaborative talk within a predictable, organized structure. I hoped that students, with a shared book as common ground, would be able to talk together on their own, interpreting and reacting to the text from their individual perspectives without my guidance. I also needed to find strategies that, while preserving freedom of choice, would lead several students to select the same book.

The first few book conferences were disappointing. Instead of thoughtful conversations, I heard brief summaries of each student's favorite part of the plot. Their talk either ended abruptly or became a discussion of the lineup for Saturday's baseball game. I theorized that questions prepared in advance by the readers might make discussions more purposeful and invite more thinking. Christenbury and Kelly (1983) posit that by asking and answering questions we reveal feelings and views for ourselves as well as for another person. "This experience," they point out, "in turn, clarifies our views and focuses our thinking" (1).

Knowing that my students would need to learn to prepare questions that could generate conversation, I developed a preliminary plan. After completing the books they were currently reading, each would draft seven questions to guide a book conference with any future readers of that book. I specified seven because that number offered a degree of choice to readers who would later select only the questions that were of greatest personal interest. In conferences with me, students "tested" the questions by responding to them themselves, then revised questions that did not lead to a full response. Finally, they copied the questions onto a nine-by-twelve-inch oaktag card and filed it alphabetically by title in one of several magazine file boxes, to await future readers. As a final step, students printed the book's title and the date next to their names on a large wall chart. Thereafter, the process would continue like a perpetual motion machine. After completing a book, students would look at the wall chart to see if the title was listed. If it was listed, they would approach the question-writer to request a conference. If the book was not listed, they would write questions for future readers.

My students learned a simple way to evaluate good questions: a question had to get another person to talk a lot. To help students write open-ended questions, I suggested they might begin with words such as *why, how, explain, if you were, what do you think about, what if, what do you suppose.* I also showed them how to "piggyback" with a follow-up question to encourage another reader to go deeper. Follow-up questions included: Why do you think that? How would you feel if that happened to you? Can you give me an example of what you mean? Do you know anyone like that character? What would you have done in that situation?

Then I made up several questions about a book that I had read aloud to the class, deliberately including some that elicited only "yes," "no," or other single-word answers. Together, we revised these to make them produce fuller and more interesting responses.

In drafting questions, it was important to avoid a question-answer pattern that would mimic a testlike situation instead of generating collaborative talk. Also, for the talk to be truly collaborative, participants in the conference needed to have equal control over its agenda. As a result, I wrote the following directions on each question card:

> Readers: Select the three most interesting questions from those written below for your conference. On the back of this card, write three things or questions that *you* think should be discussed in the conference. Remember, all the readers in a book conference should respond to the questions or topics that have been selected.

Finally, to encourage my students to read books that others had read, I ordered multiple copies of paperbacks voted by my students as their favorites for my classroom library, asked readers who completed a book to write and read aloud a one-minute sales pitch to attract other readers (Trelease 1982), and suggested that they informally spread the word about books they liked to friends.

Based on the dinner discussions with my friends, I had a good sense of the kind of natural talk that I was hoping to hear. We occasionally disagreed about the meaning of an event, the depiction of a character, or the writing itself, but we laughed a lot, too. If I forgot a character's name, even an incident, I could rely on someone else to nudge my memory. Frequently something in a book triggered the recall of a personal incident or another book, and our talk would veer off for a while in a different direction. There were times when, carried away by excitement, everyone tried to talk at once or one person would start a sentence and another would finish it.

As I listened to their conferences, I noted that my students were beginning to sound much as my friends and I did when we chatted about books. I made notes as I listened to Danielle and Jennifer:

> The readers are collaborating as they attempt to recall the storyline. Danielle is coaching Jennifer, nudging her memory. Now Danielle and Jennifer are offering different opinions and giving their reasons for them. Jennifer has become personally engaged with an episode in the book, describing a similar experience she had. The talk sounds real!

Listening in on other conferences I heard readers of all ability levels become personally involved with their books. Julie, who receives remedial help, and her friend, Miko, for whom English is a second language, often chose to read the same book. Their talk about the characters in Harry Allard's *Miss Nelson Is Missing* reveals, in Purves and Rippere's (1968) words, that they are reacting to "the world of the work as if that world were not fictional" (12):

JULIE: Would you want to be in Miss Nelson's room? Why?
MIKO (*laughing*): I want to be because I could run around the classroom. And I don't have anything to do. I just—like—play.
JULIE: I would want to because Miss Nelson's nice and sweet, and she probably wouldn't give us too much homework. Did you like Miss Swamp?
MIKO: I didn't like Mrs. Swamp.

JULIE: Well, I didn't like her because she's every child's nightmare, and she's not the nicest substitute I would have.

MIKO (*laughing*): I think that, too.

Laughter is a sweet sound in the reading class. I seldom heard it before my students began to talk about books together. Julie's interpretation of Miss Nelson as a teacher extended Miko's thinking and her language usage, as well.

Sometimes students talked about their perceptions of the setting of a story. In the following excerpt from their conversation, Xin-hua and Dominique are trying to visualize the log cabin in Elizabeth Speare's book *Sign of the Beaver*.

XIN-HUA: Well, I sort of have—like the idea it looked like Abraham Lincoln's cabin [*laughing*]. And the beds were probably on the ground, I guess. I wonder how they made the door—if they had a door. And how would they get the hinges on the door?

DOMINIQUE: Mmm. How would they get a bed? How do you bring a bed all the way from Massachusetts? Did they bring it along with wire on it? Because there was no stores?

As the two readers attempted to reconstruct the cabin, they drew both upon their knowledge of the book and on their own prior experience. But the picture of the log cabin was still incomplete, and they began to generate questions that neither could answer. Finally, stimulated by their own talk and thinking, they decided to look at nonfiction books about log cabins and went off to the library to do some research.

Listening to my students taught me some important things about the ways ten-year-olds respond to books through talk. I learned that they helped each other pronounce and use new words acquired through their reading. When discussing Jane Yolen's *The Robot, Rebecca, and the Missing Owser*, Kate asked Maura why the owser looked like a mop at one point in the story. (The owser was a creature from the planet Chameleon 111 that could change its shape at will.) Kate had encountered the word *chameleon* for the first time in this book, and she was unsure about its pronunciation. Maura helped her out:

MAURA: Well, the owser was in a grey planet or something. And he turned into trees, a fire hydrant, newspapers. He changed into things.

KATE: He was a shameleon, or something like that.

MAURA: Yeah. A chameleon.

KATE: Right. That's what I meant—a chameleon.

I also learned that my students used a kid-to-kid language, speaking in their own vernacular when interpreting characters. Fudge, the young brother in *Tales of a Fourth Grade Nothing*, was referred to by various students as "a pain in the butt," "a pain in the neck," and "a little brat."

The children also did some "second guessing," to use Purves and Rippere's term for the way readers attempt to change the way the author wrote a story. For example, they would tell one another what a book *should* have been titled or how they would change a particular character or an ending to improve the story.

When I heard students begin to relate events in their own lives to things that happened in books, I was reminded again of the talk of my friends. Danielle and Jennifer were discussing Elsie, a character in *Nothing's Fair in Fifth Grade*, whom Jennifer had described as "gross" because "she stole things and was really fat and ugly." This led her to recall a girl she had known:

> See, there was this girl—she was like—oh, how can I describe her? She had really fat lips, real fat lips, and everyone called her Chubby Lip. And at first I thought she was really uchy, but then when I got to be friends with her, I didn't think she was like that anymore.

Another discovery that I made through listening to my students talk was that the individual who had prepared a question or issue for discussion was usually the one who had more to say about it. In other words, the act of generating a meaningful topic caused students to think about it in advance of the conference. As a result, those readers had some ideas they could readily draw upon to prime the pump for more talk.

The book conferences now had the tempo and sound of real talk. My students, like my friends and I, disagreed, laughed a lot, interrupted one another, and repeated themselves. Not every question or topic on the cards led to involved discussion. There were perfunctory responses when each reader would express an idea and move on. But there were also times when comments would come rushing and tumbling out in excitement, when one reader would complete a sentence another had begun. It was then that their talk had the passionate sound of readers in collaboration.

In a letter in her literature log, Jennifer convinced me to read *Bridge to Terabithia*. I did and, like Jennifer, was moved by the story of the friendship between Jesse and Leslie, their imaginary kingdom of Terabithia, and Leslie's death. Then Jennifer and I got together to talk about the book. As we talked, guided first by her questions and then by my own, I felt more than ever before like a participant in the classroom and less like a "director." When Jennifer asked me what I thought Terabithia looked like, I described what I remembered about the illustration on the book's cover, a little clearing surrounded by very tall trees. Jennifer gently explained that I was seeing it from the "real point of view." She had pictured a "castle and a kingdom with a lot of people, with Jesse and Leslie dressed like a king and queen." I liked the way Jennifer helped me extend my literal image of Terabithia with her own imaginative one.

Now, when I talk about books with my students, I find that they will correct me on facts (their memories are better than mine) and feel free to express an opinion that disagrees with mine (much as my friends do): good signs, I think, of a reader's sense of ownership. For me, talking about *Bridge to Terabithia* with Jennifer was an integral component of my reading of the book. The questions Jennifer had written for other readers' considerations, as well as the issues I raised in preparation for our conference, focused my thinking and served as springboards for conversation. They compelled me to return repeatedly to the book in search of examples that would justify my interpretations. Listening to Jennifer's views stimulated and expanded my own thinking. And talking about a book I loved *felt* so good. I hope it is the same for the other readers in my classroom.

References

Allard, Harry. 1977. *Miss Nelson Is Missing.* Boston: Houghton Mifflin.

Atwell, Nancie. 1984. "Writing and Reading Literature from the Inside Out." *Language Arts* 61 (3) (March): 240–52.

Blume, Judy. 1972. *Tales of a Fourth Grade Nothing.* New York: Dell Yearling.

Christenbury, Leila, and Patricia Kelly. 1983. *Questioning: A Path to Critical Thinking.* Urbana, IL: National Council of Teachers of English.

DeClements, Barthe. 1981. *Nothing's Fair in Fifth Grade.* New York: Scholastic.

Forbes, Elizabeth. 1943. *Johnny Tremain.* New York: Dell.

Paterson, Katherine. 1977. *Bridge to Terabithia.* New York: Crowell.

Purves, Alan C., and Victoria Rippere. 1968. *Elements of Writing About a Literary Work.* Urbana, IL: National Council of Teachers of English.

Speare, Elizabeth. 1984. *The Sign of the Beaver.* New York: Dell.

Tough, Joan. 1985. *Listening to Children Talking: A Guide to the Appraisal of Children's Language.* London: Ward Lock Educational.
Trelease, Jim. 1982. *The Read-Aloud Handbook.* New York: Penguin.
Yolen, Jane. 1981. *The Robot, Rebecca, and the Missing Owser.* New York: Knopf.

The Teacher Interview

CAROL AVERY

AN INTERVIEW BY JANE HANSEN

*C*arol Avery began her career in education as an elementary school librarian. For the past twelve years she has taught first grade in the Manheim Township School District in Lancaster, Pennsylvania. Carol's articles about her students have appeared in the journal *Language Arts* and as chapters in *Seeing for Ourselves* (Bissex and Bullock 1987), *Stories to Grow On* (Jensen 1989), *The Whole Language Evaluation Book* (Goodman, Goodman, and Hood 1989), and *Workshop 1* (Atwell 1989). She is currently at work on a book about reading, writing, and literature in the primary grades.

I taped two conversations with Carol during the summer of 1989 while she was teaching in the University of New Hampshire Summer Writing Program and I was teaching in the Institute for Reading, Writing, and Learning, also at UNH. I cut sixty pages from the transcript of our talk, some of which was laughter, as we had a good time becoming better acquainted. We first met several years ago when Carol came to my home for the party that Heinemann gave when they published *Breaking Ground* (Avery 1985), another book to which Carol contributed a chapter.

As I culled text from the transcript I tried to find those parts that showed the essence of Carol's classroom, and I finally focused on the read-aloud times, which set the tone for her students' learning. I decided to begin with Carol telling about one of the many books that she read to her class this year.

CAROL: I read *Two Bad Ants* to my class this year.
JANE: Oh! I love that book!

CAROL: I do, too. What was interesting about the book was that the children kept negotiating its contents all year. Was it sugar or salt? Coffee, tea, or cocoa? Is this a chimney or a brick wall? Was this a kitchen or a bathroom? And then they'd say, "Well, the window is open. There's a window there so it can't be a bathroom." Then someone would say, "I have a window in my bathroom," and somebody else would add, "Yes, but the shade would be closed"—talking back and forth and negotiating the book's meaning. Every time I'd read it they'd negotiate it again.

I love the children's responses to books. I withhold interpretations of my own in the beginning because first graders are already used to the teacher as *the* authority.

JANE: They didn't think there was an exact story for that book. Lots of people, Jane Yolen (1985) for one, say there's not one story in any book. Every reader makes his or her own story. We teachers can't dictate the meaning.

CAROL: This year *Blueberries for Sal* was one of our early favorites. I realized that each time I read it they told stories about when they'd gotten lost from their own mothers. Now, I never read that story that way. I'm back in Maine thinking about picking blueberries with my boys when they were little. But they were telling their stories, and it suddenly occurred to me there are universal themes in these books. The good books are the ones kids can make identifications with. We started, then, making a list of their experiences, and I got several stories about getting lost in the drugstore or the shopping mall. Good literature touches their lives and they connect with it.

Some kids chose to write books about getting lost. In fact one of the writing strategies they talked about at the end of the year was how, when they couldn't think of a topic for writing, they'd look around the room at the books and start thinking. For example, *Where Are You Going, Little Mouse?* might remind them that we've all had times when we felt like running away. The books they connected with were the same ones they wanted to hear time and time again.

JANE: When I think back, I always read to my classes, but I didn't reread.

CAROL: Sometimes I'd read something if they'd beg me to read it again, but not like I do now. I reread and reread and reread. In fact, that's one of the things my kids will comment on. I'll ask, "How did you learn to read this book?" And they'll say, "Well, you read it to us."

This year one of the first books that several of my children chose to read independently was *Cookie's Week*. Tomie dePaola illustrated it. There's a little cat named Cookie. Monday she fell in the toilet, and there was water everywhere. Tuesday she . . . you know, one thing after the other. They love that pattern and the predictableness of it. The final lines are "Tomorrow is Sunday. Maybe Cookie will rest." They chose it for independent reading because they *knew* that book. And they loved the cat's antics. School gets so heavy and serious sometimes; there has to be some laughter.

JANE: There must be. That's true.

CAROL: In *Rumplestiltskin*, they just loved the language. "The devil told you that! The devil told you that!" They'd wait till that line to chime in—that delicious sense of being someone who's naughty. They get so involved with characters. At the beginning of the year some of them were going around the playground saying, "The devil told you that! The devil told you that!" and stomping their feet.

I encourage the kids to talk about the books I read to them. I think that talking about books as you read them is part of reading. Maybe that's because when I read to my boys, as a mother, we always talked about the stories we read.

JANE: So when you read to your first-grade class they're saying things and chiming in as your two boys did when they were little, and you read to them at home?

CAROL: Sure. Lots and lots of that.

JANE: I think a very important part of the beyond the basal movement is starting reading with entire books, as opposed to starting by learning sounds, then words, then, after you know the words, reading the story. In your classroom you're starting with the whole story.

At the beginning of the year your children often read books by telling about the pictures. Do they ever read to the class that way?

CAROL: Oh, yes, and some of those stories, at the beginning, are what we would consider pretty weak: "This, and then this. He's here, and then he's here." And they flip through the books very quickly. But it's amazing the way those stories get richer through the year, as the children hear more and more stories and as they write, composing their own narratives. Lots of reading and writing open their imaginations, and they begin to see more in the pages of the wordless picture books.

The kids were doing great stories with wordless books this

spring, like *The Grey Lady and the Strawberry Snatcher*. Molly Bang came to Millersville University and spoke, and that book became very popular. Telling the story and making it different each time was really a challenge. They'd say they got ideas from other people but, "Mine is different from Jeffrey's because Jeff did this and I did this."

JANE: Did you purposely set it up so that the challenge was to tell it differently from everyone else?

CAROL: No. They did it themselves.

JANE: Again, what we're talking about isn't just not using a basal but using books in a very different way than we used the basal stories. In a basal discussion, the children don't come together to find out what they can learn from each other, confident that each one will have found something different in that story.

CAROL: No, they don't, and that's what's so sad and so stifling to me. One of the things that makes reading to children interesting is the surprise of their responses: "Oh, I never thought of it that way!" Their reactions are so different from what we anticipate, and they make us think. The children respond based on who they are at a point in time, and that's very different from where we are.

JANE: The way you use books, you encourage them to come alive.

CAROL: Yes, and I want to see my students do lots of reading. I just had a feeling, when I used basals, that the children could do more reading, and I was amazed at what they could do.

When I moved into this approach to reading, I was teaching the class that Lori was in, in *Breaking Ground* (Avery 1985). I gave them the Scott Foresman tests, the level two for Systems Unlimited, in December. Every child in the class passed! There had been many kids in my previous classes who didn't finish level two until the end of the year.

But with Houghton Mifflin the preprimer test was different. My children had a nice sight vocabulary, but it wasn't the one on the test. But by the end of first grade, when I gave them a Houghton Mifflin test, it had worked out.

JANE: It will work out in time because your children read a lot. The sixth-grade children in the elementary school in Stratham, New Hampshire, where we just finished a research project, read an average of two books a week. By the end of the year, how in the world could they *not* do as well as if they had read one basal reader?

CAROL: So we're redefining the way we're looking at reading in our schools.

JANE: We're redefining how we're looking at reading ourselves.

CAROL: And in light of that, how does that affect how we look at it as teachers? I remember adult literature courses I took: I had a college course in contemporary poetry. We'd come in, and the professor just sat there, and he'd say, "Well, what do you think, Mrs. Avery? What do you think, Mr. Shriver?" Wonderful discussions. He taught me a lot. At the end of the course he said he had never learned so much himself in a course in all his life, and he was close to retirement.

JANE: I think that's important: the fact that as a teacher he considers himself a learner and thinks that his students have something to offer to him and to each other.

CAROL: I had a little girl who read James Marshall's version of *Goldilocks* this year and wrote a story about what happened when Goldilocks went home without the muffins that she had been told to bring. She was really in trouble—not because she'd broken into the bears' house but because she didn't bring home the muffins. The kids' interpretations of the books are so diverse. Teaching reading is waiting and listening; it's not being the authority on the book.

In a basal program, the teacher is the authority. I've come to trust the kids more. I've come to be a better observer, watching where children are and waiting and seeing and being able to identify when a kid is in a slump, and they do go into slumps. I think it's that watching, Jane, that observing, that's crucial in teaching reading.

JANE: Yes, I think it's watching. And listening. Kate Schoedinger is a fifth-grade teacher here in New Hampshire. She changed her reading this spring, and at the end of the year surveyed her students about the dissolution of their three distinct reading groups. One of them said, "You feel like a sardine in the middle group because you're stuck in the middle forever and ever and ever." Somebody else said, "It's like this. If you're in the low group you feel stupid, if you're in the middle group you feel stuck, if you're in the high group you brag."

CAROL: Oh!

JANE: No child said, "I prefer being in ability groups." So why does grouping persist? I wonder if part of the reason is because we never think to ask the children if grouping helps them. It comes back to whether we value the children's opinions and experiences.

CAROL: Ability groups always bothered me, incredibly so. I used to want to get all the children as even as I could by the end of the year, so they weren't pegged forever going through the elementary grades.

JANE: It's so true. When a first-grade teacher puts children into a bottom group, he or she isn't just putting them there for first grade. The teacher's putting them there, by and large, for the rest of their school career. But children learn more when they can use the entire class as a resource.

CAROL: This year some little boys came up to me one day and said, "We can't figure this out, and we asked Monica and even *she* doesn't know." It was the Carrick book on dinosaurs. They had a couple of possible alternative words, but none of them made sense when they read the sentence through.

JANE: When they say, "Even Monica doesn't know," you know you've set it up so that when they're reading and come to a word they don't know, they can do something about it.

CAROL: We made a long list of strategies. We talked about the things they could do, things like ask another person. They could try to sound it out, but that won't work all the time, so they might try another strategy, such as looking at the pictures for clues or at the shape of the word. Or they could read the rest of the sentence and skip the word, and they decided, "Sometimes you have to come back to it and sometimes you don't."

JANE: Because you don't need to know how to read every word in order to understand a book.

CAROL: Right. That's important for them to know. We filled four sheets of chart paper with strategies.

JANE: So they really are articulate about what it is they can do.

CAROL: Very much so. Taking away the basal unmasks children's learning processes. There's a wide range of strategies out there, and I see that one of my tasks is to help children identify them.

JANE: What we want the children to know, then, is that there's no recipe to follow. What they need to learn are options, to talk so that they're aware of various things they might try.

CAROL: They'll talk about choosing books. I have to say that at the beginning of the year some of them had a hard time finding a book that they could manage. Finally, I talked to them one day after we'd read several versions of Goldilocks and the Three Bears. I said they could get a book that was "too hard" or a book that was "too easy" or one that was "just right."

JANE: That's perfect.

CAROL: It worked very, very well. I'm always exploring options with them, always asking them, "How did you learn to do this?" As I move around the room I talk to kids, and I jot down things they say. I keep folders on them, and I mark down what they're doing—if they self-correct, for example. Or if they stop and say, "That doesn't make sense," I watch what they decide to do at that point. I also listen for the comments they make to me or to their classmates. Just little notes on the kinds of things they do or what I observe as they're reading something to me.

JANE: So let's say you're walking around your room and the children are here and there reading. They're under the desk . . .

CAROL: You've got it.

JANE: . . . or on a pillow by the window. They're reading books of their choice. I know you wouldn't always say the same thing, but you stop beside a child who is alone, and that child is in the middle of a book. How might you begin your conversation?

CAROL: If the child is reading along smoothly I might say, "What's this about right now?" Sometimes they just start talking to me.

JANE: Yes, because they're used to you stopping.

CAROL: Right. Or I might ask, "What's the best part you've read?" or "What do you think is going to happen?" Or I might ask them to read a little part to me. In the beginning they want to do a lot of that, and that's important as they're getting into reading, to hear themselves read to others as well as to themselves. It's almost like a writer needs the audience at a conference. The beginning reader seems to need an audience, too.

JANE: What if you stopped beside a child who isn't reading along fluently?

CAROL: I might say, "How's this coming?" and then, "Read a little bit to me." Particularly in the beginning of the year, we would probably point to the words and read together, and then I'd drop out and come in as I felt he needed me, out and in, out and in. If he can manage it on his own, okay, but if he continues to need support, then I might suggest, "Why don't you read this with so and so?" or I might say, "Elizabeth, John needs a teacher. Would you come be John's teacher? I know you've read this book." And John beams. I don't know that I've ever found a child who's found that to be a put-down. They're just so delighted, "Oh! Somebody's going to read with me!"

JANE: Isn't the reason they accept this partly because that's not your only use of reading in pairs? Children can read in pairs almost whenever they want, and they're not paired only because someone needs help?

CAROL: Sure. They stop and talk about books together all the time.

JANE: Well, now, let's say you're walking around and you stop beside a pair, or maybe a trio. What might you say?

CAROL: They would probably start telling me how it's going. "We were doing da, da, da, and Elizabeth thinks da, da, da, but *I* said. . . ."

JANE: That sounds like what they do when you read to them, like when they bantered about *Two Bad Ants*.

Do your children meet in groups other than these informal groups of two or three?

CAROL: At the end of the year, I started bringing kids up to talk about books they'd read in groups of three or four, just having discussions about those books, which was like a mini-version of the whole-group discussion. I didn't find that the small groups were quite as crucial except that it did help some of the more reticent children find a voice.

JANE: And that happens with adults, too, in my classes. Some talk more comfortably in small groups.

CAROL: And so I'd bring groups up and I'd say, "Well, tell me about this book. You've all read this one at different times." (I don't have enough copies in the room to have five kids read one story at the same time and then talk about it.)

JANE: They have each read a particular title, one after another. They don't need to all read it on the same day.

CAROL: No, they don't. I think that gets into basalizing children's literature. You can easily get into the trap of deciding, or asking kids to decide, "This group of kids is going to read this book."

JANE: And we can basalize the responses we ask of children. I remember the way we used to teach reading, the way I used to teach reading, when we had them come and read a little bit, and we listened to find out how well they were doing. We asked standardized questions to find out if they comprehended the story.

CAROL: That's a group based on evaluation of reading rather than engagement with reading.

JANE: Yes! We want to engage them in books.

Now, in these little groups they talk about a book they've all read. So, if I were to go into your classroom I wouldn't see a group who'd come together, each with a different book?

CAROL: You would. They do that on their own, too. Frankly, I've been so busy and the spread of my children's abilities is so great that I haven't had time to organize response groups, to set up the management of it. I haven't done it, and I haven't seen a particular need to, but I might if they were second graders. The books in our classroom are part of the history of our community. Most of the books they've read are ones that I've read first some time during the year because I read so many hundreds of books to them. But I can anticipate that as they get older and are reading longer and longer books, that probably wouldn't be true any longer. It was beginning to happen in my classroom at the end of the year.

Children were beginning to be the first person to have read a particular book. I would hear them telling somebody, "You really should read this book. This is a good thick book." I remember overhearing Josie, after she had read Aliki's *The Two of Them*, a book about a grandparent and a child. Some of the girls had gotten into Tomie de Paola's *Now One Foot, Now the Other* and *Nana Upstairs & Nana Downstairs*, and Josie was running around telling all the kids who had liked those books that they would also like this one.

JANE: So to understand how your children read is to understand how much interaction goes on in the classroom.

CAROL: There's talk about books and authors all the time.

JANE: This interaction is interesting to me because at Stratham, the two researchers in the fifth and sixth grades kept saying that in order to understand how reading works you can't come in and listen only to a whole-class share, or only when the children are sitting there reading, or only to a small group. Those are the official parts of the reading program, but you've got to come before school and during snack because there are so many times when books are talked about. That's when the children, oftentimes, share what a book really means to them and pass on ideas to each other: "This is one you have to read next." That's when they have books on their minds.

CAROL: And lines from books come out in their talk all the time. They've got me doing it. They would tell me to do something and I'd say, "What do you want me to be, a rat of all work?" like Templeton.

JANE: Did you read *Charlotte's Web* more than once?

CAROL: Twice. I begin every year with it. We make a list of the novels I read aloud, and at the end of the year I have the kids choose one for me to read again, and every year every class has chosen *Charlotte's Web*.

JANE: How many of these ways of using books are the same each year?

CAROL: Every year is a little different. Right now I'm more conscientious about reading a lot to the children, about never letting that get shoved aside.

We're talking books all the time. I can say to my kids, "Where's such and such a book?" They'll say, "Oh, over in such and such a bucket," and somebody runs and finds it. They know where every book in the room is. They keep track of them because the books are such an integral part of their environment.

One day at the end of June it was steaming hot, and we had all the windows open. All of a sudden this rainstorm came, and Jody said, "Look, listen to the rain!" And Stacy grabbed our new book *Listen to the Rain* and read it aloud.

If they're living the books all the time, those connections come out. They're immersed in literature—the language, the characters, the storylines—and it just becomes a part of them, both individually and collectively as a community. The literature becomes the language of our community, the language everybody knows, because they have heard these books again and again.

References

Aliki. 1979. *The Two of Them*. New York: Greenwillow.

Aruego, Jose, and Ariane Dewey. 1986. *Where Are You Going, Little Mouse?* New York: Greenwillow.

Atwell, Nancie, ed. 1989. *Workshop 1: Writing and Literature*. Portsmouth, NH: Heinemann.

Avery, Carol. 1985. "Lori 'Figures It Out': A Young Writer Learns to Read." In *Breaking Ground: Teachers Relate Reading and Writing in the Elementary School*, ed. Jane Hansen, Thomas Newkirk, and Donald Graves. Portsmouth, NH: Heinemann.

Bang, Molly. 1980. *The Grey Lady and the Strawberry Snatcher*. New York: Four Winds.

Bissex, Glenda L., and Richard H. Bullock, eds. 1987. *Seeing for Ourselves: Case Study Research by Teachers of Writing*. Portsmouth, NH: Heinemann.

De Paola, Tomie. 1973. *Nana Upstairs & Nana Downstairs*. New York: Putnam.

———. 1981. *Now One Foot, Now the Other*. New York: Putnam.

Goodman, Kenneth S., Yetta M. Goodman, and Wendy J. Hood, eds. 1989. *The Whole Language Evaluation Book*. Portsmouth, NH: Heinemann.

Jensen, Julie M., ed. 1989. *Stories to Grow On: Demonstrations of Language Learning in K–8 Classrooms*. Portsmouth, NH: Heinemann.

McCloskey, Robert. 1948. *Blueberries for Sal*. New York: Viking.

Marshall, James. 1988. *Goldilocks and the Three Bears*. New York: Dial Books.

Martin, Bill, and John Archambault. 1988. *Listen to the Rain*. New York: Henry Holt.

Van Allsburg, Chris. 1988. *Two Bad Ants*. Boston: Houghton Mifflin.

Ward, Cindy. 1988. *Cookie's Week*. New York: Putnam.

White, E. B. 1952. *Charlotte's Web*. New York: Harper & Row.

Yolen, Jane. 1985. "The Story Between." *Language Arts* 62 (6) (October): 590–92.

Zelinsky, Paul O. 1986. *Rumplestiltskin*. New York: E. P. Dutton.

CHILDREN AS AUTHORITIES ON THEIR OWN READING

BOBBI FISHER
Josiah Haynes School
Sudbury, Massachusetts

*T*here are no ditto sheets or workbooks, no basal texts, no ability groups, no readiness or "letter of the week" programs in my kindergarten. My teacher's editions are *The Foundations of Literacy* (Holdaway 1979), *The Art of Teaching Writing* (Calkins 1986), and *Reading, Writing and Caring* (Cochrane et al. 1984). My consumables are paper and pencils, my reading books are trade books, and my tests are the children's work over time.

Each half-day kindergarten session begins with the entire class participating in shared reading for about half an hour. This time is spent discussing and dramatizing songs, poems, chants, trade books, and big books, all of which are written in enlarged print so that the children can see the text as I point to it. We talk about print concepts, letters, and sounds in context and as the need for skills arises. Independent choice time follows when the children are required to read and write. They select what they want to read: big books, small predictable books, trade books, story tapes, or the shared reading charts on which I've printed familiar songs, poems, and chants. Writing workshop rules are also simple and open ended: draw a picture of your own choice, write something (ranging from scribbles to sentences), put your name on the paper, and stamp the date.

The children also select from a variety of nonassigned activities in the room. They play at the sand or water tables, build with blocks, explore math manipulatives and play math games, paint, construct with recycled materials, build at the work bench, and play in the environmental area, which changes throughout the year to become an aquarium, a veterinarian's office, a greenhouse, a post office, a bank, and so on. Writing and reading occur naturally within all the activities.

At the end of the school year I wanted a better understanding of what the children felt they had learned from my reading program. I wanted to evaluate the program from their point of view. I recalled Don Holdaway's comment that "children have many things to teach us that are very difficult to learn from textbooks" (1979), that teachers should be humble before children, valuing their understanding of their own learning. And so I decided to conduct an interview with each student, asking the children to evaluate themselves as readers. In this way I could more formally document their observations of themselves as learners in my classroom. I prefaced the interviews by telling students that I was continually learning ways to be a better teacher, and that they could help me by describing what had been important to them as readers during their year in kindergarten. Then I met with the children individually and asked them eighteen questions about their reading.

My questions fell into three categories: general questions ("How did you learn to read?"); specific questions ("Did you learn more about reading from shared reading or independent reading?"); and questions about my role as teacher ("What did I do in school to help you read?"). I used a questionnaire to record their answers and also tape-recorded the interviews. Over the summer I transcribed each interview, then recorded the responses on a data base. Next, I evaluated each child's responses in relation to formal and informal assessments I had conducted throughout the year, studied the children's writing folders, and reviewed the evaluations of letter and sound knowledge I had conducted in September and April. I also reread anecdotal notes I had written during the year and tapped my memory for incidents not written down but memorable because they were so powerful.

At the end of my research, I identified six characteristics that were important to the children and, consequently, the reading program. Taken together, they led me to realize that the children were most successful and happy when they understood their own reading abilities and could participate in choosing how to use and strengthen them. In a sense the children told me that they learned best when viewed and treated as authorities on their own learning. My role was to create an environment that encouraged authentic reading and writing and to watch for opportunities to support their reading development and teach new concepts and strategies.

All the children considered themselves readers.

I had planned to start each interview by asking "Can you read?" but as soon as I began with my first subject, Miranda, I realized that this was a poor question. The quizzical look on her face said, "Why are you asking me that? Of course I can read, you know that." So I deleted the question. For the remainder of the interviews I talked to the children as readers, and they responded as readers, just as they had every day in class since the first few weeks of school.

How did their "I am a reader" attitude develop? I knew the children hadn't entered school thinking of themselves as readers. My September assessment records indicated that I had no independent readers. In response to the interview question "Could you read before you came to kindergarten?" only three children said that they could, qualifying their response by mentioning specific books.

Donald Graves (1983) writes that only fifteen percent of children entering kindergarten say they can read. An incident that occurred early in the school year during our shared reading time supported this statement but also demonstrated that teachers can help give children confidence that they are readers.

"Raise your hand if you can read," I instructed the class. A few tentative hands went up. "Who can read *Brown Bear, Brown Bear*?" Now, every hand waved in the air. "So who can read?" All the hands stayed up as smiles widened across the children's faces. By this third week in September they had read the book many times and had illustrated their own copies to take home and share. Jeremy had even read *Brown Bear* over the telephone to his uncle in Oregon.

From that moment, the children in my class were readers and writers. They had joined what Frank Smith (1988) calls "the literacy club." They read the daily schedule on the blackboard to find out if we were going outside to play; they wrote me a note asking me to get red paint for the art area; they posted a *clozd* sign on the architect's office and expected everyone to read and abide by it; and they wrote reports for the classroom aquarium and read them while acting as tour guides for parents and children from other classes. Reading and writing became a natural part of their day.

Six-year-old Monique summed it up in her response to the last question in the interview, "Do you think everyone in this class can read?"

"Don't know anyone that can't," she replied. What impressed

me most about her response, as well as those of the other children, was its matter-of-fact tone. I thought I was asking a deep
and subtle question, but the children showed me that the answer
was obvious. They reinforced what Frank Smith (1983) has been
saying for years: "You learn to read by reading."

All the children felt they learned to read by reading a lot.
"You try, and try, and try, and you do it."
  "I kept reading it and reading it."
  "I tried and got better."
These were typical responses to the question "How did you
learn to. read?"
When asked the name of her favorite shared reading book,
Sally immediately mentioned *The Birthday Cake* and added that
she read it every day. I remembered reading it with her through-
out the year, watching her evolution as a reader through that
favorite book.
The same message, that they had learned to read by reading,
surfaced in response to my question "What have I done in school
to help you read?"
"You read to us and we listened."
"You read to me and then I heard the story once and I sort
of memorize some of the words. When I am reading I can think
back and know what the word is."
"You read to us again and again."
"You teached us a lot of books like *Brown Bear, Brown Bear.*"
"You taught us at the rug."
I had expected more specific answers that would put me at
the center of the children's learning, focusing on what I had
done: pointing to the text when we sang and read big books,
writing on the little post-it notes when we innovated a text, rereading a line when we came to an unknown word, masking
letters and words in context to focus on graphophonics. The
children had enjoyed these interactions with the text and were
able to talk about the strategies in context. When they read to
me, I observed them using some of them, but I did not see them
practicing the strategies when reading independently during
choice time. As they said, during that time they "just read." I
discovered that my demonstrations had enabled the children and
their responses to books to take their place at the center of the
reading program.
Why didn't the children mention the teaching moments? I'm
still looking for answers. Perhaps if I had asked more specific

questions, such as "Did pointing to the words when we read a big book help you as a reader? How?" instead of "What did I do in school to help you to read?" the children could have given more specific answers.

Children created strategies to help themselves read.

The children indicated that they understood some of the specific things they did that had helped them to read; these were as varied as the number of students:

"By moving my lips."

"I learned to write first."

"I did my upper- and lowercase letters."

"By reading words from the big books."

"I learned that I don't have to do it real; you just think what it says by the pictures."

"Letter and pictures" was what Anna said had helped her. In my September assessment I had learned that Anna could not name one letter, although she wrote her name perfectly. She came to kindergarten an emergent reader (Holdaway 1979): she could retell a story and weave her own story into her lively, detailed drawings. Her mother told me she had not had much time to read aloud at home since Anna had three teenage brothers and sisters and four younger siblings, including twins. What Anna needed was to hear lots of stories, so I spent the year "doing bedtime story" with her. We snuggled up together on the rug, alone or with friends, and enjoyed books much as I had with my own children. We looked at the pictures, talked about the story, commented about print concepts, and talked about letters and sounds.

During writing workshop Anna drew many pictures and for most of the year wrote the letters in her name, sprinkled with numbers she knew, in various sequences. By the end of the year she was writing a few beginning sounds, could recognize half of the letters, and could distinguish letters and numbers. It is no wonder she referred to "letters and pictures" when I asked her about her reading. Both were important to her during the year, not in isolation but in rich contexts, and she summed up my role in her growth as a reader by saying, "You sit down with us."

Paul, on the opposite end of the spectrum, mentioned that "sounding out" had helped him to read. Where did he get that idea? During shared reading we had talked about letters and sounds in context and focused on beginning consonants to help us predict and confirm, but I had never emphasized "sounding out."

Paul had an uncanny ability as a speller; he could spell all the states and their capitals. In fact, he could spell better than he could read. When he came to a word he didn't know, he would spell it and then read it correctly. I recalled how he had used this procedure to come up with the word *checkered* when reading *Caps for Sale*. "Spelling out" would have been a more precise term, but that wasn't in his vocabulary. I guessed that Paul had spent a lot of his time spelling words to himself during shared reading, and I hadn't realized it until the interview.

Anna and Paul exemplify the ways that children developed personal strategies, within the framework of the reading program, to help themselves become successful readers. A structured, commercially packaged program would not have given Anna and Paul the same opportunity to develop personal strategies and learn to the full extent of their abilities. Most kindergarten basal programs focus primarily on letters and sounds. Paul already knew the letters and sounds and was using that knowledge in context as a successful reader, while Anna needed to hear stories and learn to use letters and sound knowledge in context.

Each child was aware of where he or she was on the reading continuum.

One of the most informative questions I asked was "Can you read a book you have never heard before?" The children's answers—"No," "Don't know," or "Yes"—corresponded exactly to my assessment of their individual reading stage. My students knew they were readers, but they also knew the extent of their abilities.

To assess students' individual progress as readers, I apply the stages of development described by Don Holdaway (1979, 1980) and the stages on the reading continuum outlined by Cochrane et al. in *Reading, Writing and Caring* (1984). About once every two weeks, each child picks a book (usually a big book) they know and like and, using the pointer, reads it to me. I record their current reading stage, evaluate the reading strategies they use, and plan further instruction from there.

The children who answered "no" when asked if they could read a book they had never heard before were those whom I had previously identified as emergent readers. In reading to me they felt success and displayed confidence with familiar books they chose. They read fluently, pointed very generally to the print, and approximated the text from memory. They focused on meaning and sentence structure. They did not attend to the details of print, displaying what Cochrane refers to as "graphophonic transparency."

The children who indicated that they didn't know if they could read an unfamiliar book were those I had assessed as early readers, at the bridging stage on the reading continuum. As they read familiar, simple texts such as *Hairy Bear* or *Mrs. Wishy-washy*, they pointed word for word, very slowly, as if glued to the print. Memory of the text helped them focus on graphophonics. Their understanding of reading was changing so rapidly, and they were so involved in the process, that they really *didn't* know if they could read new material.

Those who said that they could read an unfamiliar book were advanced early readers, at the take-off stage on the reading continuum. They could work through a new simple text or a more difficult book they had heard only a few times. They were becoming more fluent, and they practiced a lot. When they read to me they worked hard to use all three cueing systems—syntactic, semantic, and graphophonic—in harmony.

I also observed that although all the children considered themselves to be readers, they reacted differently in different reading situations and with different materials. When they participated as group members during shared reading they were natural risk-takers, engaging in free-flowing approximations and community laughter and experiencing intense joy in the story. During independent reading, they displayed many of the same characteristics but with softer voices and one eye peeled to make sure that no one was watching. When they read one-on-one with me, the tone changed again and often depended on my reaction; risk-taking was more self-conscious, approximations more calculated, laughter more subdued, and joy in the story shifted to joy in reading "success."

Family influences were important to many of the children in learning to read.

"I read to my mom and she told me the words I didn't know."
  "My mom kept reading books to me."
  "My brother taught me."
Many of the children referred to family members in learning to read. They talked about the process as a joyful one with

bonded adults—moms, dads, and siblings. Ellen continually referred to her older brother during our interview, just as she had in numerous conversations throughout the year. Undoubtedly he was a very important person in her life, and as far as she was concerned, he was her primary teacher.

Don Holdaway (1979) and Gordon Wells (1986) have documented the powerful literary influence of the home environment: where children and adults enjoy stories together, where the same story is read over and over, where concepts about print are talked about in context, where children have opportunities to practice being members of "the literacy club."

The importance of family that children demonstrated in the reading interviews has motivated me to do more to bridge the gap between literacy in the home and the school. Next year we'll ask older brothers and sisters to read to the class. We'll invite younger siblings for a story hour. And we'll encourage parents, grandparents, aunts, and uncles to read and write with us in the classroom.

The children benefited from a variety of reading routines and procedures.

"I like to read with a friend."

"I learned to read by reading *The Birthday Cake* every day."

"I learned best from the big books."

I wanted to discover if there were specific routines and procedures that the children preferred. Had they learned more from shared reading or independent reading? Had they learned more from reading by themselves or with a friend?

About half the children indicated that they liked a variety of approaches, but some did have preferences. Karen, Anna, Miranda, Keith, and Billy were clear in their choice of shared reading. They were emergent readers who sat right up front during shared reading and showed intense delight in rereading all our big books and singing our favorite songs. They relished the demonstration, as well as the participation that is in full voice during this time.

Monique and Paul indicated that they benefited more from independent reading than shared reading. They were advanced early readers, serious about this business of figuring out reading. They relied heavily on graphophonic cues and read slowly, word by word. They sensed the power in reading a favorite book over and over again. They wanted to practice, and they wanted to take off.

"I usually read with a friend. I read to Mark," reported Nicky, another of the advanced early readers in the class. Learning to make friends was the most important part of school for Nicky, and he had learned a lot about friendships by reading to Mark, an emergent reader. They would sit on a chair and "do bedtime story" together. Mark and Nicky were teachers for each other.

Stephen, another advanced early reader, told me in his usual serious manner, "I like to read by myself because my friend would ask me questions, but by myself I could just concentrate on the book."

These children taught me the importance of offering a variety of daily routines and opportunities for reading: shared reading, independent reading alone, or independent reading with a friend. A commercial reading program would not have provided for the variety of routines and choices of materials that were so important to the children in my class. Instead it would have set one daily routine for the whole class or for small groups of children based on ability. The children would have spent a large portion of their school day using prescribed materials, with the expectation that they would progress sequentially within the structure of the program. Although Nicky and Mark were on different reading levels, they were learning from each other, and Stephen was flourishing because of the choices he was able to make.

My interviews with the children demonstrated the importance of a program that enables children to think of themselves as readers, gives opportunities for them to read extensively in a variety of ways, recognizes and encourages the influence of the home, helps children become aware of their strengths as readers, and allows them to develop individual reading strategies at each stage through which they pass. The interviews also taught me that my kindergartners were genuine experts on their own learning.

Interview Questions

I have listed the interview questions and noted in parentheses some of the changes I anticipate making next time around. At the end of next year, undoubtedly I will make new revisions.

1. Can you read? (Next year I won't ask this question since all of the children thought of themselves as readers.)
2. How did you learn to read?
3. What did we do in school to help you read? (Instead, I'll ask what I did to help them read, and I'll ask more specific

questions, such as "What did you learn, or do, when I pointed to the text during shared reading?")

4. Which helped you most, the songs and charts, the big books, or both?
5. Which was the most important big book (or chart) for you? Why?
6. What other big books were helpful to you?
7. Which big books can you read?
8. What other books can you read?
9. Did having to read a book during work time every day help? How?
10. Did you learn more about reading from shared reading, from independent reading time, or both?
11. Did you learn to read more from reading by yourself or with a friend?
12. Can you read a book you have never read before?
13. Could you read before you came to kindergarten?
14. Do your parents know that you can read? How do they know?
15. Can you write? (Again, since all the children thought of themselves as writers I won't ask this question next spring.)
16. Which can you do better, read or write?
17. Did writing every day help you to read? How?
18. Do you think everyone in this class can read? Write? How do you know?

References

Calkins, Lucy M. 1986. *The Art of Teaching Writing.* Portsmouth, NH: Heinemann.

Cochrane, Orin, Donna Cochrane, Sharen Scalena, and Ethel Buchanan. 1984. *Reading, Writing and Caring.* New York: Richard C. Owen.

Cowley, Joy. 1980a. *Hairy Bear.* Story Box in the Classroom: Stage 1 series (1984). San Diego, CA: The Wright Group.

———. 1980b. *Mrs. Wishy-washy.* Story Box in the Classroom: Stage 1 (1984). San Diego, CA: The Wright Group.

———. 1986. *The Birthday Cake.* Story Box in the Classroom: Stage 1 (1984). San Diego, CA: The Wright Group.

Graves, Donald H. 1983. *Writing: Teachers & Children at Work.* Portsmouth, NH: Heinemann.

Holdaway, Don. 1979. *The Foundations of Literacy.* Portsmouth, NH: Heinemann.

———. 1980. *Independence in Reading.* Portsmouth, NH: Heinemann.

Martin, Bill, Jr. 1982. *Brown Bear, Brown Bear.* New York: Holt, Rinehart and Winston.

Slobodkina, Esphyr. 1940. *Caps for Sale.* New York: Scholastic.

Smith, Frank. 1983. "Learn to Read by Reading." In *Essays into Literacy: Selected Papers and Some Afterthoughts.* Portsmouth, NH: Heinemann.

———. 1988. *Joining the Literacy Club: Further Essays into Education.* Portsmouth, NH: Heinemann.

Wells, Gordon, 1986. *The Meaning Makers: Children Learning Language and Using Language to Learn.* Portsmouth, NH: Heinemann.

WRITING AND READING LITERATURE IN A SECOND LANGUAGE

DOROTHY M. TAYLOR
Edith C. Baker School
Brookline, Massachusetts

*I*f someone wrote about me in a book, I'd want to read it. That's why I understood Elena's squeal of delight as she pointed to her sister Maya's book on the shelf in my classroom. She knew she was an important character in the book because Maya, a sixth grader, had taken it home to read to her family the night before. Elena and a small group of first graders sat in a huddle on the rug and listened intently as I read Maya's book entitled *About My Family* (Figure 1). I was as pleased as Elena with her sister's first book because when Maya began the school year she spoke no English. In fact, Maya burst into tears if an English-speaking adult even looked at her. Now she had become an author as well as a role model for her younger sister and her peers.

Maya knew that her story would become a book because I had shown her class samples of last year's books before she started writing. The English in these texts was beyond her at this point, but she did understand that her book would be added to the pile and shown to the next person who hadn't yet written one. In other words, she had an audience. If Maya realized that her words were lacking in entertainment value, she knew her "voice" came through clearly in her illustrations.

It soon became evident that Elena and I weren't the only people in the classroom reading Maya's book. Just as more literate students borrow stylistic devices from professional authors and classmates (Atwell 1987), Maya's classmates borrowed her pictorial device of X-ing over a picture to express a negative, a universal symbol understood by readers everywhere. Several stu-

Figure 1   Maya's Book "About My Family"

My father's name is Boris.

My sister's name is Elena.

Figure 1   continued

dents later incorporated this quick and clever symbol into their own stories (Figure 2).

I shouldn't have been surprised to discover that my students were heartily devouring each other's books, picking here and choosing there to create their own masterpieces—which someone else would then borrow and bend to create another masterpiece. Limited English speakers have few reading options available to them, particularly the older English as a Second Language (ESL) student. I teach ESL in a K–8 school, and throughout my professional career I have struggled to find appropriate reading materials for my beginning students. I encourage my students to write from day one no matter how limited their English, but I've had a great deal of difficulty initiating a reading program in the upper grades. The abridged, rewritten versions of classics listed in the ESL catalogues offer so much less than the originals that I can't bring myself to use them. The short readings in ESL texts are usually long on theme, but short on plot and style. My seventh and eighth graders grow tired of picture books written for younger children and endless rounds of fairy tales and fables.

While I was busily searching for appropriate reading materials outside of the classroom, my students had already found a solution *inside* the room. After their pieces of writing were completed, the children and I typed, illustrated, and bound them into books. The finished products were celebrated with an in-class reading, then taken home to be read to family members. Upon return, the books were placed on the "New Works" shelf where students were free to read them whenever the class wasn't involved in whole-group instruction. It was these books that the children turned to as models of topic, theme, and style. Peer authors, like Maya, shared not only similar interests and concerns but also the same vocabulary and syntax limitations. Even the newest arrival could understand Maya's first book about her family, enjoy it, and draw on it in crafting his or her own first book—which explains the seventeen versions of *My Family* that sit together on the classroom bookshelf.

"Writing is the foundation of reading; it may be the most basic way to learn about reading," writes Jane Hansen (1987, 178). The ways in which my students borrowed from each other when writing were tangible signs that they were reading each other's books, not as a classroom exercise in decoding but to incorporate the stories into their mental storehouse of how to convey meaning with a limited amount of English.

I do not have any sisters and brothers.

When Diana was born the dog got lost.

Then I told him the truth, but he said that I would get a vacation, raise, work for two weeks, and then I would be FIRED!!!

*Figure 2   Using the X.
A: From Anna Gothart's
"My Family." B. From
Rita Rosenblit's "My
Family." C. From Maxim
Fleisher's "Smokey's
Story."*

Much of the early borrowing that my students did involved pictures rather than words. Symbols are an important means of expression for ESL students because of the thrifty way they convey embedded meaning, so it is not that surprising that an abundance of flags, flowers, and, especially, hearts made their way into the students' books. Sometimes these symbols appeared as little more than pictorial clichés; however, to the ESL writer or reader they could represent meaning beyond that which words express (Figure 3).

Two symbols that became popular with the students were drawings of books as beginning and ending signifiers. Leads and conclusions might have been beyond their linguistic capability, but conceptually the children knew that beginnings and endings are marked. Iriena first used a picture of a book to signify the end of her story *My Little Rabbit*. Sasha, who arrived two months later, used an open book at the beginning of her story and a closed book at the end. The open/closed book quickly became a standardized way of expressing the beginning and end of a story

Figure 3   Use of Symbols. A: From Rita Rosenblit's "My Family."
B: From Leonid Kruzinsky's "My Dogs."

and was learned in the same way and for the same reason that young children begin stories with "Once upon a time"—because stories they had read and like begin that way.

While some students clung to the open book/closed book method of beginning and concluding stories, Andy designed his own ending signifier. On the last page of his first book, entitled (surprisingly) *My Family*, he added a waving hand with the words "Bye! Bye!" inside it. Maya, always on the prowl for new avenues of expression, used this idea to conclude her next book but refined the hand with fingernails and a ring. Andy, in a final show of one-upmanship, concluded his next book with more details (knuckles) and more rings.

At the beginning I found the students' pictures to be the most joyous and creative part of their books. However, they were eager to use words to express themselves and were mindful of the role that classmates' books could play to help them in this area. The first attempts at modeling usually involved pretty straightforward sentence structures: *My name is . . . , I am . . . , I have a. . . .* The importance of these simple statements should not be overlooked since this was personal information that children were providing their peers. For example, Andy's book *TV Shows* was important because it described programs that Andy liked rather than the preferences of some anonymous textbook author. *TV Shows* was also important because Andy began every sentence in his book with "I like." This repetitious sentence pattern served as a model for other children's books about the things that they liked and a guide for sorting out the complexities of written English.

Figure 4 is an excerpt from Maya's book *Things That I Love* that I've translated into Russian (Maya's native tongue) to demonstrate how repeated patterns contribute to reading in a second language. With careful examination a reader could probably figure out that "I" is expressed by the symbol Я (pronounced *Ya*) in Russian, люблю equals love, and книги are books. If a Russian speaker were to pronounce the words, the reader would be well on his or her way to decoding the Russian graphophonic system—in addition to recognizing about six vocabulary words. Syntactically, the reader might have observed that verbs follow subjects (*I love*), and that Russian punctuation and capitalization are similar to English. The reader would draw on background knowledge of English (using phonics, context clues, and assumptions about standard spelling and syntax) to put meaning into the Russian text.

Figure 4   Maya's Book "Things That I Love"

Similarly, ESL students bring what they know about reading in their native language to a text written in English. Background knowledge varies with each student, but their age, reading ability in their native language, and the nature of their native language are all factors that influence the transfer of reading skills into a second language. For example, Chinese students, who use an ideographic system of writing, might recognize the importance of memorization but not how phonics work, while the Spanish student who knows how to sound out words to decode becomes frustrated with the many irregularities in English spelling. Student-authored books were the result of successful efforts to incorporate previously learned reading and writing conventions with new knowledge about English. Students reading these books didn't consciously set out to learn a specific set of skills, but the availability of interesting texts at and above their language levels combined with the requirement to create their own texts led them to improve their reading and writing ability.

The transfer of literary knowledge was not limited to the basic skills of reading. Sasha was reassured about the value of simile and metaphor after I gushed over her poetic language in *Russian Winter*.

> It is winter in Russia. Winter is a beautiful and merry season in the Soviet Union. Everybody is eager for the winter to come.
> The snow is falling and covering the black ground like a white fluffy tablecloth.
> The trees lose their leaves and lonely, they fall asleep, hoping that their dreams will be very good, and they will continue to sleep until the spring comes. . . .

When she followed up with a story about spring, Sasha borrowed from herself, carrying her "white fluffy tablecloth" with her as a security blanket of sorts. *Spring in the Soviet Union* reads:

> Spring is also a very beautiful season of the year in the Soviet Union. The winter is gone. The white fluffy tablecloth has disappeared but instead beautiful small brooks appear.
> Trees wake up from a long winter dream. In this season they aren't alone because on the trees buds appear, little grass grows and birds sing song. . . .

Most of my students this year came from the Soviet Union. They received support in their native language from a vivacious and competent Russian bilingual teacher. As the ESL teacher, I worked with all of the school's nonnative speaking students to develop English language skills. In addition to the Russian students, this year's crop included students from Finland, Hong Kong, Taiwan, and France.

A close bond generally develops among ESL students because of their similar experiences in adjusting to a new language, culture, and school. The ties were, understandably, even closer among the students from the Soviet Union. In addition to a shared language and culture, each of the students had just completed the same long journey from the Soviet Union. Mainly for bureaucratic purposes the trip included a stop in Vienna, a longer stay in Italy while they awaited U.S. entrance visas, then on to New York, and finally a last hop to Boston. These students arrived bursting to tell of their travel adventures, especially about their two or three months in Italy. A travelogue genre quickly emerged, with titles including *My Travels in Italy* and *My Adventure in Italy* and descriptions of the museums and monuments in Vienna and Rome. Because of the shared immediacy of the topic these books were widely read. The children enjoyed reading about places they had just been to, but this shared knowledge also opened their critical eye. Andy wanted to know how Vlad could have written about Italy without mentioning the ice cream. His book, written after Vlad's, included mouth-watering details about the flavors and taste of Italian ice cream. By reading each other's books the students learned to recognize the good in a text but also to recognize the shortcomings.

Early works of new arrivals tended to be fairly egocentric, even when interspersed with pictures that were clearly meant to entertain and amuse. In addition to the ever-present *My Family*, early titles included *My Apartment, My Clothing, My Friend*, or simply *My Life*. Usually, by the third or fourth book the student was ready to branch outside of his or her own world a bit; in other words, they grew bored. At this point, I often suggested fiction. Graves (1989) tells us that the children in his and Jane Hansen's reading and writing study "felt that a child who wrote fiction, even with shared names, had crossed an important line into authorship" (55). My students welcomed the invitation to step through the fiction barrier; some, like Iriena, didn't wait for an invitation but crashed on through. Iriena, a spunky eighth grader, completed her first book, *My Little Rabbit*, at the end of October. Halloween was the topic of the day so she took advantage of the holiday to create her first piece of fiction entitled *Halloween*.

La-La!

Today is Halloween!

Sisters Anna and Olya go to their friend's. Her name is Oto. She is 5 years old. Anna and Olya are 4 years old.

Anna is a cat, Olya is a witch. Anna is wearing an orange sweater, orange hat and orange tail. Olya is wearing a black hat and yellow nose. She's wearing green face paint. Oto is a rabbit. She is very beautiful.

Happy Halloween girls!

Iriena edited and put together the book in record time so that she could get it on the shelf while Halloween was still hot among the readers in her classroom.

Sasha arrived at our school in early November, just as Iriena was completing *Halloween*. Sasha had studied English for many years in the Soviet Union and arrived with a fairly sophisticated knowledge of the language. Iriena and Sasha immediately became close friends and shortly after Sasha's arrival Iriena started to work on a new short story. "Shhh, it's a secret. It's for Sasha," Iriena told me, glancing at Sasha as she pulled the first draft out of her notebook. She had obviously worked a long time and used her Russian/English dictionary extensively to produce the story. We worked together to make the English understandable, and about three weeks after completion of *Halloween*, Iriena published *Sasha and Sara*, a much richer piece of fiction because of her desire to appeal to the reading ability and taste of her more accomplished friend.

It was morning, Sasha woke up. The little curly dog lay on the porch. Sasha went to him. Topsy (it was the dog's name) jumped up and licked Sasha's face.

It was summer. It was Sasha's favorite time of the year. It was morning, but Sasha pushed Topsy aside earlier than usual, because she wanted to go to her favorite friend's Sara. . . .

Many of my students were enthusiastic about reading in their native languages, and I encouraged them to do so. I also urged them to read in English as soon as they had the language ability to understand and enjoy material written at their age level. Neither I nor they looked upon their published books as a replacement for literature by professional authors in their native tongues or in English. However, the student-authored books did serve an important role in helping beginning ESL students view reading and writing in English as a process in which meaning is actively constructed rather than passively received. To construct that meaning the students learned about written English, its standard spelling, syntax, and vocabulary. They also learned to appreciate the importance of literary and rhetorical devices, recognize genres in literature, and critique a literary piece. The knowledge that these students gained as readers of each other's texts is information that they brought to the reading of works by professional authors; it was a bridge that connected them to the literature of their new language.

References

Atwell, Nancie. 1987. *In the Middle: Writing, Reading, and Learning with Adolescents.* Portsmouth, NH: Boynton/Cook.

Graves, Donald H. 1989. *Experiment with Fiction.* The Reading/Writing Teacher's Companion series. Portsmouth. NH: Heinemann.

Hansen, Jane. 1987. *When Writers Read.* Portsmouth, NH: Heinemann.

BEYOND LABELS: TOWARD A READING PROGRAM FOR ALL STUDENTS

JOAN LEVY
RENA MOORE
Pelham Elementary School
Pelham, Massachusetts

*R*ENA: This year Ms. Levy and I will both be your teachers during reading time.

NICK: Will I get to work with Ms. Levy?

JOAN: Each of us will work with everyone in the room.

Most of our second and third graders knew both teachers and accepted our new arrangement for teaching reading. They did not know the reflection, soul searching, discussion, and planning that had led us to take a team approach. We hoped some long-established roles would become blurred: we wanted the students to see us as their reading teachers, not as Ms. Moore the classroom teacher and Ms. Levy the special education teacher.

RENA: We are all readers in this room.

JOAN: Some people can read very well, and some are just beginning to read, but everyone can read.

RENA: And we can all help each other to learn more about books and reading.

Team teaching succeeds when both teachers share common beliefs about children and learning, trust in each other's skills and judgment, and openly discuss both the strengths and weaknesses of the team. After seven years of observing each other's teaching styles, we felt we could work together in all of these areas. Over those years the special education program had evolved from a resource-room base to a special-needs group taught within a regular classroom. Now we were secure enough as teachers and colleagues to integrate all students into the learning community of Rena's regular classroom, a grade 2–3 combination.

We were convinced that team teaching would alleviate the problems of segregation and stigmatization associated with special ed, pull-out programs. When Joan had tried working with special education students as a separate group within the regular classroom, she found that the children had difficulty generalizing skills to a large-group setting and feeling part of the classroom community. We felt that our teaching together, as a team, would allow for the best possible integration of skills for special education students, provide them with role models in the form of more capable readers, and expose all the students to a diversity of personalities, learning styles, and teaching techniques.

Developing children's confidence in their abilities was one of the secrets we discovered in teaching beginning readers. All preschool children believe that they can learn to read, but after several years of limited success, some second and third graders have lost hope of ever being able to read. One of the first questions Joan asks a child receiving special education services is, "Are you a reader?" Often the child will respond, "No." For both of us, one of the strongest indicators of the success of our program was the day Seth came in and announced, "I am a reader."

JOAN: On the shelves you'll find a wide variety of books at all different levels. Everyone will be able to find a book to read, and you'll have time every day to read books to yourself.

RENA: Each of you will also have a reading partner for paired reading time. Remember to select a book that you can read and that you think your partner will enjoy. You might want to practice reading your chosen book during our silent reading time.

We ensured that every child could find an appropriate book to read by stocking the classroom library with plenty of predictable and wordless books as well as selections from the first-grade classroom. Rhodes and Dudley-Marling (1988) provide an excellent bibliography of predictable trade books for the primary classroom. We also found that many of the second graders had read books from the Story Box series and were glad to see such old favorites as *The Big Toe* on the shelf in their new classroom.

We envisioned a program rich with a "balanced set of literary experiences" to ensure that each learner had "substantial opportunities to engage in real reading and writing activities" (Allington and Broikou 1988). The morning reading period of one hour and thirty minutes included silent reading, group discussions of books and stories, projects based on books, writing about books in journals, reading conferences with a teacher, and "paired reading" or reading to a friend (Koskinen and Blum 1986; Topping 1989). Leaving little to chance, we staged a role-play to demonstrate what should happen in our version of paired reading and covered all of the problems we thought the students might encounter:

RENA: Where should each pair read?

JOAN: Wherever they like in the classroom as long as both partners are comfortable and don't bother another pair.

RENA: What should each partner read?

JOAN: A good book that a friend would like.

RENA: What should the partner do while the other partner is reading?

JOAN: Listen to the story.

RENA: What if the book is too hard?

JOAN: Politely suggest selecting an easier book or ask that each partner take turns reading the book.

RENA: What if you can't hear or don't understand the book?

JOAN: Politely tell your partner.

We assigned students to work together based on their reading levels and social skills: one member of each pair was a little stronger reader, and the other was more cooperative and sharing. During paired reading time, we circulated around the room, listening to the children and providing encouragement for their efforts.

We knew that children read more when they could select their own books about topics that interested them. Over the years we had found that elementary students are often intrigued by animals, and this group was no exception. From the school library and the resource room we selected books about animals that represented a broad range of reading abilities. Some of the books had controlled vocabularies and short, simple sentences (Granowsky 1983, 1986a, 1986b). We acknowledged to each other the limitations of these texts but felt we could overcome them through examining and discussing the illustrations with the children, providing other books, and recognizing students' own background knowledge.

RENA: You'll notice that we've put out some new books about animals on the library shelves.

JOAN: We know that many of you like animals and might like to learn more about them.

William, a student who had received special education help in reading for one year, began to read book after book from several different wildlife series (Hogan 1979; Bevington 1983; Collins 1987). He had stopped repeatedly reading the same book and had moved along, in his own progression, to repeatedly reading the same style of book written by one author. He found a pattern that was comfortable for him as a reader in books that supplied him with plenty of facts with which to impress his classmates. We were comfortable letting him continue in this pattern, secure in the knowledge that when he was ready, he would move on to new books and authors.

In February William was ready to move on. He selected *Mysterious Castle Builders: African Termites* as his next book and decided to write a report about termites for his project. His termite report wove together information from his reading with knowledge about animal adaptation that he had discovered during the class's science unit. He proudly shared it during writing time, and his peers' questions reflected that they recognized him as the class expert on termites:

RYAN: What does the queen look like?

WILLIAM: You won't believe it. She's huge, thousands of times bigger than the other termites.

ELENA: Do people eat termites?

WILLIAM: They do in Africa, raw or fried. Maybe Australia.

JOSH: What is cellulose?

WILLIAM: It comes from wood or plants.

JOSH: You know a lot about termites.

We didn't need to reward the students with stickers for their reading. They rewarded themselves and each other through the work they accomplished, the recognition they received, and the genuine praise they gave. Students were accepted and valued as individuals.

Not every beginning reader progressed as rapidly as William. For some, even the simplest text was too difficult. We decided to use the "neurological impress" (Tunnell and Jacobs 1989) or prerecorded reading method (Chomsky 1976, 1978; Carbo 1981) with these children. Joan tape-recorded herself carefully and slowly reading a text. A student would listen to the tape recording while following along with the book and then try to read the book silently without the tape, and finally read the book to one of us. This process was repeated two or three times. Seth made slow but steady progress with this approach; he continued to need to listen to a tape several times before he could read the book without it.

In March Seth read *The American Bison,* a book from the Endangered Species of America series, aloud to Joan. Perplexed, since this book was not on tape, she asked him if someone else had read the book to him. "No, I read it by myself. I just knew the words." Seth had made the transition from nonreader to reader. Although reversals still plagued him, he had learned to use context and background knowledge to compensate. He also had his area of expertise: when his social studies group read about the life of the Plains Indians, only Seth knew that bison was another word for buffalo.

When we looked back over the year, we realized that the classroom had served as a literate environment for all of our students. Each child had made progress over the year, and all but one of the children receiving special education services showed at least two years' growth in reading in the Gates-MacGinitie test mandated by our school district. Average growth for all the children in the class was over two years. But we need to continue to look at several issues.

The Individual Education Plan (IEP) sets goals and objectives for children who receive special education services. As the special education teacher, Joan had primary responsibility for implementing each child's IEP. We felt we were closely following the goals and most of the objectives of the IEP but often through indirect methods. Rhodes and Dudley-Marling recognize the dilemma of the special education teacher who is attempting whole language approaches and suggest alternative phrases and objectives for an IEP: "the learner will spontaneously correct 80 percent of any reading miscues that don't make sense" rather than "the learner will pronounce the first one hundred words from the Dolch Word List with 80 percent accuracy."

Time is an age-old problem of all teachers but particularly for those who team-teach. There was never enough planning time to develop units, share insights about students, or toss around new ideas. There was also never enough classroom reading time. It was a standing joke in our class that "things were just getting good" when the class had to leave for gym or art or music. Often our only salvation was that writing time followed the special subjects, and many projects begun during our reading period could be completed then.

Because of her caseload, Joan was only able to be in the classroom for an hour of each day's reading time. She was present for individual reading conferences and group discussions of books and stories but missed silent reading, most of paired reading, and writing. Optimally, we would have cotaught all of these areas; in the best of all worlds, we would have cotaught all day.

We began the year with a theoretical foundation for our work together as teachers of reading and a great deal of confidence in our ability to integrate regular and special education; we also had some trepidation about the day-to-day coordination such teamwork would take. Now we have begun to note our successes.

We succeeded in alleviating the confusion that many special needs children feel as they change environments and teachers, since the regular classroom remained their learning environment throughout the year. Their frustration over dealing with different teacher expectations lessened as we became more conscious of our differences and either established one set of expectations for all or made our own requirements explicit. Joan rediscovered the broad range of abilities in a regular classroom, and Rena discovered strategies to use with students with learning difficulties. Through a literature-based curriculum and heterogeneous grouping the children experienced the joy of reading and the excitement of learning together through reading. For most special education students this was a new experience as these elements are missing from pull-out programs that concentrate on teaching isolated skills. We did teach reading skills, but within the context of meaningful books and topics selected by our students. The skills that we taught were determined by individual students' needs, not by a preordained scope and sequence, and these needs often crossed regular education/special education boundaries. Not only did the beginning readers thrive in this classroom but the "average" and "gifted" readers also benefited as each one's needs and interests were met. A reading program that goes beyond the basal can incorporate all learners.

References

Allington, Richard L., and Kathleen A. Broikou. 1988. "Development of Shared Knowledge: A New Role for Classroom and Specialist Teachers." *The Reading Teacher* 41:806–11.

Bevington, Jeff. 1983. Animals on the Move Books. San Diego, CA: The Wright Group.

Carbo, Marie. 1981. "Making Books Talk to Children." *The Reading Teacher* 35:186–89.

Chomsky, Carol. 1976. "After Decoding, What?" *Language Arts* 53 (3) (March):288–96.

——. 1978. "When You Still Can't Read in Third Grade: After Decoding, What?" In *What Research Has to Say About Reading Instruction*, ed. S. J. Samuels. Newark, DE: International Reading Association.

Collins, David. 1987. Beginning to Read Books, Set R. Cleveland, OH: Modern Curriculum.

Granowsky, Alvin. 1983. Real or Make Believe Series. Cleveland, OH: Modern Curriculum.

——. 1986a. Endangered Species of America Series. Independence, OH: Schoolhouse.

——. 1986b. Endangered Species of the World Series. Independence, OH: Schoolhouse.

Hogan, Paula Z. 1979. *The Life Cycle* Series. Milwaukee, WI: Raintree Childrens Books.

Koskinen, Patricia S., and Irene H. Blum. 1986. "Paired Repeated Reading: A Classroom Strategy for Developing Fluent Reading." *The Reading Teacher* 40:70–75.

Lisker, Tom. 1979. *Mysterious Castle Builders: African Termites.* New York: Contempory Perspectives.

Rhodes, Lynn K., and Curt Dudley-Marling. 1988. *Readers and Writers with a Difference: A Holistic Approach to Teaching Learning Disabled and Remedial Students.* Portsmouth, NH: Heinemann.

Topping, Keith. 1989. "Peer Tutoring and Paired Reading: Combining Two Powerful Techniques." *The Reading Teacher* 42:488–95.

Tunnel, Michael O., and James S. Jacobs. 1989. "Using 'Real' Books: Research Findings Based on Literature Based Reading Instruction." *The Reading Teacher* 42:470–77.

Wright Group. 1980. Story Box in the Classroom: Stage 1 series. San Diego, CA: Wright Group.

APPRENTICESHIP: AT FOUR OR FOURTEEN

LINDA RIEF
Oyster River Middle School
Durham, New Hampshire

I slipped into the window seat, buckled my seat belt, and waited for the remaining passengers to board. A little boy and his father sat down next to me. The boy crawled up into the middle seat and waited for his dad to buckle him in. I smiled, then turned back to the window.

"Are we off the ground?" the little boy asked me.

"Not yet," I answered. "What's your name?"

"Jimmy," he said. "I'm four." And he held up four fingers. "Are we in the sky yet?"

"Not yet," I said.

When we reached cruising altitude he watched as his dad unbuckled his own seat belt. Jimmy unbuckled his, climbed down, and maneuvered his way in front of me so he could see out the window. I asked his dad if it was okay. He nodded, leaned back against the cushion, and closed his eyes.

Jimmy asked questions, seldom waiting for an answer. "Do the wings flap? What holds us up? Where's the pilot? What are clouds made of? Are we there yet? Are we above the trees? Above the biggest mountains? Why's the sky blue?"

When he tired of my answers he returned to his seat and told me his story. His mom and dad were "'vorced." He'd been visiting his mom in Boston. He could count to one hundred. He and his mom had built a snowman in her yard.

I held my journal in my lap. When Jimmy asked me about it I explained it was a notebook in which I wrote down things I heard or saw—things that mattered to me, things I wanted to remember. "Would you like to write too?" I asked. When he said yes I ripped several pages from my journal and handed them to him with a pen. He wrote quietly while I wrote. When I looked over, he was finished (Figure 1).

"Can you tell me about your writing?" I asked.

"This is the snowman I built with my mom," Jimmy said. "This is the head," he continued, pointing to the round circle with two dots and a mouth. "These are the bodies. This is the nose," he added, pointing to the carrot. When he tried to explain what they used for eyes, I couldn't understand the word. In frustration he began to draw. He pointed to the tree on the paper and said, "From oak trees. You know, the seeds of oak trees."

"Oh, *acorns*," I replied.

"Right," he said.

"Could you write the word *snowman*?" I asked.

"Sure." Jimmy drew an *M*, covered it with dots, framed it with a circle, like his other story parts, and handed the piece to me.

"Nice," I said. "What are these dots?"

"Snow," he said, looking at me as if I should know that. "S-N-O-W-M-A-N," he explained, tracing the flake-covered *M* with his finger.

"Of course," I said.

Figure 1   Jimmy's Snowman Story

Jimmy continued drawing while I wrote in my journal. Between drawings, he'd look up and say, "I know how to count to a hundred. Want me to count to a hundred?"

"Sure," I'd reply, not paying much attention. He must have counted to a hundred a hundred times. Each time I'd say, "Wow! That's great. You sure know how to count to a hundred." He'd lean back into his drawing and start counting all over again.

I bent over and pulled a book of poetry from my briefcase: Paul Janeczko's *Strings: A Gathering of Family Poems.*

"What's that?" Jimmy asked.

"It's a poetry book."

"What's POTE-TREE?"

I explained that poetry was a special kind of writing. That poets wrote what they knew or wanted to know more about and shaped the words the way they wanted them to be read. I showed Jimmy several poems, pointing out the titles and telling him that's what poets called their poems. He turned back to a blank piece of paper and was quiet for a long time. The plane began to descend on its way into Minneapolis, so Jimmy stopped writing. When I glanced to my right again, I was surprised at what I saw. "What did you write?" I asked.

"Pote-tree," he said proudly. Jimmy read: "One one. Two twos. Three threes. Four fours. Five fives. Six sixes. Seven sevens" (Figure 2).

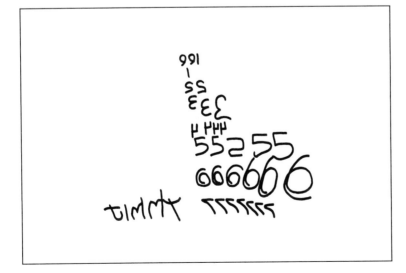

Figure 2   Jimmy's Poem

"Wow! You got all the way to seven sevens," I said. "That's a wonderful poem about numbers. Have you thought of a title?"

"What do you mean?" Jimmy asked.

"What could you call your poem? What's it about?"

"It's about one hundred," he said, looking at me like, you know that.

"Where would you write that, if you wanted to?"

"Right here," he said, and he added it above his first line.

"Can you sign your name to that, like the poets did with their poems?" I asked. Jimmy wrote his name. As we taxied to the gate I told him that my sons were in college now and seldom sent me any writing. Would he mind if I kept his drawings for my refrigerator? He agreed. All the way off the plane he kept telling his dad, "She's putting my POTE-TREE on her refrigerator." I didn't hear his dad's response.

What did Jimmy know by the end of that ride? A lot. He knew how to tell a story. He knew how to write what was important to him: building a snowman with his mom. He wrote what he knew about: numbers. He knew that writing consisted of marks on paper: pictures, numbers, and letters. He knew that the marks made sense to him, the writer, and he knew that sometimes he had to add information so the marks made sense to a reader. He knew how to write a word—his name—and how to combine drawing and letters when he didn't know a whole word (an *M* covered with snowflakes). He knew what a title was for. He understood the concept of genre: in this case poetry and its unique arrangement on a page. He even knew how to use writing to teach someone something they don't understand—a tree to get at the word *acorn*. Jimmy is a writer, reader, speaker, and listener. Jimmy is four years old.

I met Jimmy five years ago. Every September since then, thoughts of Jimmy have helped me to trust my eighth-grade students. Instead of filling my classroom with grammar texts and expurgated literature anthologies designed by publishers who don't trust kids or teachers to know, I see that I am doing the same thing in the classroom that I was doing on that airplane: immersing myself in writing and reading and sharing it with my students. I trust students to read and write in their own voices, to teach me what they know, and to come up with writing that is worthy of the refrigerator. And I am more aware than ever that what I choose to do in the classroom is a guide for what my students choose to do.

In *More than Stories* Tom Newkirk (1989) argues that "children can adopt a variety of written forms in addition to the story and that they do so by attending to the demonstrations of written language surrounding them" (24). Jimmy knew a lot about literacy—but I can't be sure what he knew before the plane ride. I am fairly sure he did not know about poetry. But he could attend to the poetic form because of the demonstration he was involved in. Children apprentice themselves to us when we read and write for authentic purposes. That's what I want them to do. That's what Jimmy did; that's what Tricia does.

A month after completing eighth grade, Tricia sent me a packet of her writing. The large manila envelope contained two letters, one a month old; a short piece of fiction; and a play. Tricia's first letter shows that she identifies with me as a writer, not just her teacher. But she also needs response to her writing, to better see what's working or not working. She knows I will respond honestly.

June 26

Dear Mrs. Rief,

How is your summer going? I saw your piece in the N.H. Alumnus magasine. I really like the way you started it talking about taking notes on anything and everything. The pieces you included that you had written were great. I think the thing that most people will come away remembering is this line . . . "For a moment, I am the writer who teaches. I can feel the difference."

The thing that really prompted me to write this letter to you is the fact that I'm stuck. There's a piece I wrote in 6th grade that with some revisions I'd like to send to Merlyn's Pen. The problem is I need a reason for the old man to be at the railroad station. Or maybe some inner conflict that he's trying to work out by writing. I'm thinking that possibly I could include the fact that there is obscurity and a strange type of silence that comes from being in a crowd. Since you know the most about writing of the people I know and since you have a head full of ideas I thought I'd ask for help from you. It may be because I had to submit so many pieces to you or for what ever reason but I'm never embarrased to have you read my writing. Actually I think it's because you never just say "that's a good piece Tricia."

. . . thank you for your time. If you have any ideas please send them to me. And thanks for your patience reading my scribbles and alterations.

Appreciativly, (is that a word?)
Tricia Crockett

In her second letter Tricia has made an important decision. She will be a writer. She is the observer of everything around her: comments by teachers, quotes on the board, thoughts from her reading. And she is keenly aware of audience. The fiction piece is going to *Merlyn's Pen*. The play might be for just her grandmother. All the writing is for her.

July 21

Dear Mrs. Rief,

Thank you for inviting me to the workshop/class today at UNH. It reinterested me in my own writing. And I've made an *important* decision. Nothing in my life will restrain me from being an active writer. Sounds simple enough, but it also means that I *will* be a *published* writer.

I have to be. What else could I be when I can sit and talk for hours with teachers (even in the summer) about writing and find it *so* interesting.

My family (especialy now that my brother has graduated) turns more and more often to me asking what I want to be doing after High School. I always reply that I haven't thought about it. I know it's a lie but I say it. I somehow thought that a writer wasn't a . . . a . . . established enough profession/dream. But *now* I'll answer with my real dream.

Please thank for me one of the teachers in the class today. He was one who had had my folder, he was trying to decide if he wanted to teach 7,8 or 8,9. Physical description? Blond, had a mustache. A coment he made about how I shouldn't quit next year and about how diverse my folder was helped me to decide.

If I'm going to thank him I should also thank you for all the encouraging things you've said over the year. I should also thank Mr. Schiot. He made a comment to my mom yesterday about how my writing had a force to it already that he as an adult hadn't acomplished. All these gave me a confidence and corage to make the decision.

Remember how we once talked about how the Upper Peninsula of Michigan is full of Scandanavians. Here's a true story of the stubborness of them from when my grandmother went up for a 50 year class reunion this summer.

Family Polotics
A Play . . .

. . . Yes, Mrs. Rief, it actually happened. My grandmother has never liked her ex-inlaws so it became the highlight of her trip . . . That didn't come out bad for a first draft . . . I'll copy it over and do some work on it. If nothing else my grandmother will get a kick out of it.

Anyway, thank you again. I meant to say also that I like the quotes you had on the board. Here's one from a book called *The Flame Trees of Thika.* "But after awhile I think the pursuit of freedom only turns one into a slave." There are so many pursuits of which that could be true.

Appreciatively,
Tricia Crockett

P.S. I've just rewritten it and it's already getting better.

In my reply, I responded to Tricia's writing, pointing out what I liked and what I wondered about. I sent her a copy of *Writing Down the Bones* (Goldberg 1986), a book I use in courses with teachers. And I wrote: "Remember Donald Murray, the professor who was in the magazine with me? He says, 'Good writing makes a reader think or feel. The best writing makes the reader think AND feel.' That's what your writing does, Tricia. He gave me a sign that reads: NULLA DIES SINE LINEA. It's Latin for, 'Never a day without a line.' Writing takes confidence and courage—getting published takes patience. It all takes a lot of words on paper. You have it all."

Tricia replied that week.

August 7

Dear Mrs. Rief,

I got your package today. Thank You! I've read one chapter of the book and I'm already excited about it. I'm sure I'll be underlining and scribbling in margins.

Since woodshop in 6th grade I've had a block of sanded wood with a fancy edge on it. Tonite I wood burned the saying in Latin that you gave me into it. It's now on my desk.

I haven't heard from Byrd Baylor. It turns out that all her books aren't in stock in local stores so I'm going to have to order "The Desert is Theirs." I *really* (notice the correct spelling) want it now that I've visited Arizona. It turns out I was glad I did that writing-reading project on the West right before going out. I noticed more things that way. After a lot of work I'm going to send "Ghostwriter" to Merlyn's Pen. Thanks for your advice and the book. Till the next time,

Tricia

Tricia is a reader, writer, speaker, and listener. Tricia is fourteen years old.

Jimmy and Tricia taught me that I am not a silent partner in my classroom. I guide and direct my students by what I do and what I choose to immerse them in for reading and writing. In three hours Jimmy had apprenticed himself to me as a learner. He wanted to do what I was doing. Tricia, too, wants to do what real learners are doing. She apprentices herself to those teachers who are reading and writing and learning with her.

I wasn't reading a basal on the flight to Minneapolis. I wasn't filling in purple ditto sheets with context-stripped words—*cat, tree, girl*. I had no dot-to-dot books available to occupy Jimmy's time. I shared what I was doing as a learner and for my purposes, not intentionally modeling my learning but sharing my authentic reading and writing with him, trusting that he would get what he could from it. I had no idea he would understand so much.

I do the same thing in my classroom. I had no idea Tricia would understand so much.

References

Goldberg, Natalie. 1986. *Writing Down the Bones.* Boston: Shambhala.

Janeczko, Paul B. 1984. *Strings: A Gathering of Family Poems.* New York: Bradbury Press.

Newkirk, Thomas. 1989. *More than Stories: The Range of Children's Writing.* Portsmouth, NH: Heinemann.

Rief, Linda. 1989. "Fragments of Language: A Conversation between Texts." *New Hampshire Alumnus* LXV (4) (Summer): 4–6.

CALL FOR MANUSCRIPTS

---

*W*orkshop is an annual about the teaching of writing and reading. Each volume is centered around a theme and features articles by teacher-researchers of grades K–8, reports of first-hand observations that show a teacher in action and include the voices and writing of students and/or colleagues. Contributors are paid. The editor is currently soliciting submissions for the third and fourth volumes.

The theme of *Workshop 3* is The Politics of Process. It is intended to help teachers introduce and gain acceptance for process approaches to writing and reading. The editor invites administrators as well as teachers to submit articles to this volume. *Workshop 3* will feature such topics as: curriculum design that supports the development of reading and writing abilities; evaluation procedures that show what children can do; evaluation of teachers who use a process approach; new ways of defining, observing, and recording literacy skills; and approaches to public relations that help administrators, colleagues, and parents understand and support process-based instruction. Again, the focus will be on new work in these and related areas. The deadline for *Workshop 3: The Politics of Process* is August 1, 1990.

Workshop 4 will address The Teacher as Researcher in the 1990s. Teachers from across the United States and Canada participated in the birth of an alternative research tradition during the last decade. Rather than viewing themselves solely as consumers of others' research, classroom teachers began to ask questions about how and why their own students were learning. And rather than attempting to establish the tight controls of quantitative modes of inquiry, teachers drew upon ethnographic philosophies and methods. They observed in their classrooms, documented their observations, and wrote about what they had discovered as members of the classroom community. The published insights of teacher-researchers have made an important contribution to our knowledge of language learning and to the development and refinement of sensible new ways of teaching language.

Workshop 4 will explore new questions and directions for teachers' research in the next decade. Such issues might include but are not limited to: the role of talk in literacy; relationships between drawing, drama, writing, reading, and talking; multi-genre writing and reading; writing and reading across the disciplines; the writing and reading of special needs, gifted, and ESL students; the role of the teacher's expectations, literacy, or scholarship; and research collaborations between a teacher and students. *Workshop 4* will extend the theories and models described in such texts as *Understanding Writing* (Newkirk and Atwell 1988), *Seeing for Ourselves* (Bissex and Bullock 1987), and *Reclaiming the Classroom* (Goswami and Stillman 1987). The deadline for *Workshop 4: The Teacher as Researcher in the 1990s* is August 1, 1991.

Manuscript Specifications for *Workshop*

When preparing a manuscript for submission to *Workshop*, please follow these guidelines:

* Contributors must be teachers of grades K–8 (with the exception of *Workshop 3*), and submissions should be written in an active, first-person voice ("I").
* Contributions should reflect new thinking and/or practice, rather than replicate the published works of other teacher-researchers.
* Submissions must adhere to a length limit of 4,400 words per article (approximately 12½ pages typed double-spaced, including illustrations and references).
* *Everything* in the manuscript must be typed double-spaced, including block quotations and bibliographies.
* References should be cited according to the author-date system as outlined in *The Chicago Manual of Style*.
* Graphics accompanying manuscripts must be camera ready.
* Manuscript pages should be numbered consecutively.
* Send two copies of the manuscript to the editor at the following address:

Nancie Atwell
Editor, *Workshop*
Dogfish Head
Southport Island, ME 04576

- Include a cover letter indicating for which volume of *Workshop* the manuscript is to be considered, as well as the author's school address, home address, home phone number, and grade level(s).
- Enclose a stamped, self-addressed manila envelope so the manuscript can be returned, either for revision or for submission elsewhere.
- If the manuscript is accepted for publication, the author will be required to secure written permission from each student whose work is excerpted.

This call for manuscripts may be photocopied for distribution to classroom teachers. The editor invites all interested teachers of grades K–8 to consider sharing discoveries about teaching and learning in the pages of *Workshop*.